News Media and the Finan   I0046629
Crisis

This book explores how leading news media responded to the 2008 financial crisis and its aftermath, showing how journalists regularly framed discussions about post-crisis regulatory reform in ways that reinforced the same market liberal policy paradigm that had ushered in the crisis.

Drawing on an analysis of nearly three years of news coverage and on interviews with journalists who covered the financial crash for major media groups, Adam Cox demonstrates how this framing of issues, often focusing on the costs of tighter regulation rather than the preventive benefits, formed the basis of a post-crisis narrative in the United States that undermined the role of the state, despite the wreckage that had just occurred. He looks at how state actors, think tanks and the financial industry worked in concert to encourage such a narrative, ultimately lending support to a market liberal worldview that was being seriously challenged for the first time in decades. While highlighting journalists' ability to resist agenda-building efforts by powerful actors, this book offers a methodology for considering media narratives based on quantitative analysis of framing patterns.

News Media and the Financial Crisis is aimed at students and researchers working at the intersection of communications, journalism, political economy and public policy.

Adam Cox is a Senior Lecturer at the University of Roehampton, where he teaches classes on journalism practice and theory. Before working in academia, he was a journalist. His career included a 20-year stint with Reuters, where he held several senior editorial roles in Europe and Asia. He has covered many of the biggest financial stories of the past 30 years, including the European currency turmoil of 1992–1993, the launch of the euro and the 2008 financial crisis.

Routledge Focus on Communication and Society

Series Editor: James Curran

Routledge Focus on Communication and Society offers both established and early-career academics the flexibility to publish cutting-edge analysis on topical issues, research on new media or in-depth case studies within the broad field of media, communication and cultural studies. Its main concerns are whether the media empower or fail to empower popular forces in society; media organisations and public policy; and the political and social consequences of the media.

Reporting China on the Rise
Yuan Zeng

Alternative Right-Wing Media
Kristoffer Holt

Disinformation and Manipulation in Digital Media
Information Pathologies
Eileen Culloty and Jane Suiter

Social Media and Hate
Shakuntala Banaji and Ramnath Bhat

The Construction of News in a Polarised State
Lessons in Maltese Advocacy Journalism
Adrian Hillman

News Media and the Financial Crisis
How Elite Journalism Undermined the Case for a Paradigm Shift
Adam Cox

For more information about this series, please visit: https://www. routledge.com/Routledge-Focus-on-Communication-and-Society/book-series/00RFCS

News Media and the Financial Crisis

How Elite Journalism Undermined the Case for a Paradigm Shift

Adam Cox

R Routledge
Taylor & Francis Group

LONDON AND NEW YORK

First published 2022
by Routledge
4 Park Square, Milton Park, Abingdon, Oxon OX14 4RN

and by Routledge
605 Third Avenue, New York, NY 10158

Routledge is an imprint of the Taylor & Francis Group, an informa business

© 2022 Adam Cox

British Library Cataloguing-in-Publication Data
A catalogue record for this book is available from the British Library

Library of Congress Cataloguing-in-Publication Data
A catalog record has been requested for this book

ISBN: 978-1-032-01263-6 (hbk)
ISBN: 978-1-032-01264-3 (pbk)
ISBN: 978-1-003-17794-4 (ebk)

DOI: 10.4324/9781003177944

Typeset in Times New Roman
by MPS Limited, Dehradun

This book is dedicated to the memory of Victor Antonie, Stephen Brown, Charlotte Cooper and James Saft.

Contents

Illustrations

Acknowledgements

This book is based on a doctoral thesis. I am indebted to my supervisors, Tim Markham and Justin Schlosberg, for their unstinting support. Judith Broadbent, Kevin Burchell, Juan Pérez González, Alison McClintock, Gary Merrill, Annabelle Mooney, Chris Roberts, Steve Schifferes, Anne Senior, Jane Simmonds, Jane Thomas and Sean Tunney all offered valuable advice along the way. And thanks go to family and former colleagues from newsrooms around the world.

1 Putting post-crisis journalism into perspective

For millions of people, the 2008 financial crisis was not just a time of hardship and loss. It was also an eye-opening moment. It showed that something as obscure as financial regulation could have an enormous and direct impact on people's lives. It demonstrated that markets could be capricious and dangerous, despite conventional wisdom which for years had portrayed them as fair and reliable. The suddenness and severity of the crisis suggested that the institutions meant to protect the financial system had been negligent, captured or both. The prospect briefly loomed of a paradigm shift towards a more interventionist regulatory policy approach.

Relying on the state to set stricter guardrails, however, means relying on expertise. As much as the crisis had opened peoples' eyes to the unpredictable nature of markets, it also sowed doubts about depending on "experts." These were the same people, the thinking went, who had got the world into such a mess. They also had not sounded the alarm. "Once the crisis had happened, not many people were willing to listen to what academics had to say, especially economists, since I think the economics profession was sort of caught up in it for failure to warn everybody," Robert Litan, a senior fellow at Brookings Institution, told me. "Who's going to listen to us?"[1] Litan believed the crisis represented the start of a society-wide distrust of expertise.

It was not just the banking industry, the academic community and the state that apparently had failed society. So too had the press. The crisis prompted fresh scrutiny about its ability to perform its traditional watchdog role. Why had journalists not seen or reported on the myriad financial problems that were mounting? The pre-crisis coverage was, by many accounts, an epic miss. Perhaps more importantly, what lessons did journalists take on board afterwards? This book explores that last question. Focusing specifically on elite news media behaviour, it examines the coverage of post-crisis regulatory reform in the United States. By elite

DOI: 10.4324/9781003177944-1

media (Chomsky 1997; Golan 2006), I mean national or international news providers that have what Guy Golan has called an inter-media agenda-setting function, meaning their editorial choices set the pace for other media.

The book offers a framework for viewing regulatory news coverage, based on different ways that journalists, and the sources they used, framed the subject of market oversight. Often this meant focusing on the costs of regulation rather than any preventive benefits. The narratives that emerged in the initial post-crisis years lent support to a market liberal worldview just when it needed it most – as it was being seriously challenged for the first time in decades.

Watchdogs and paradigms

Since its beginnings roughly a century ago, the field of journalism studies has questioned the performance of the press in its role as a watchdog for society. To begin with, there is the matter of who, or what, the press is watching out for. As James Curran wrote: "The principal democratic role of the media, according to traditional liberal theory, is to act as a check on the state. The media should monitor the full range of state activity, and fearlessly expose abuses of official authority" (Curran 2002, p. 217). Yet this prompts a question as to what happens when the state shrinks its role and outsources work to other institutions. In the United States and Britain, for example, the loudest political drumbeat since the 1970s had called for a reduced state role. Should the watchdog role therefore encompass what the state leaves to the private sector? A wider role definition – given neoliberalism's emphasis on private-sector solutions to public problems – calls on the press to monitor both public and private sector spheres. Curran alludes to this, writing that the traditional view "fails to take account of the exercise of economic power by shareholders and managers" (2002, p. 219).

As the range of activities requiring monitoring widens, so too do the external pressures brought to bear on the press. One telling statistic comes from Robert McChesney and John Nichols (2010), who cited data showing that at the time of their writing there were four public relations practitioners for every working journalist in the United States. That compared with ratios of about two-to-one in 1990 and 0.75-to-one in 1960.[2] The growth of the PR industry is one of many forces that can influence press behaviour. There may be oblique displays of power through media ownership or commercial pressures, or sociological factors such as the level of workplace diversity or the degree of interdependency in journalist-source relations.

Numerous studies have considered these dynamics and suggested journalists may not be as independent as they like to think. This critical tradition examines the ways hegemonic forces can extend to media production and compromise the notion of a free press. One of the best-known examples is the propaganda model by Edward Herman and Noam Chomsky (1988); it contends that such forces set the parameters for what is considered fit to print. But John Corner (2003) also noted that the ideas underlying this model had ample precedent. He argued that much of European media enquiry since the 1960s has focused on questions of state and market dynamics and how they influenced journalism.

One could choose from a wide variety of pressing issues or significant events – from electoral politics to corporate malfeasance – to consider the scope for news media to act as an independent check on powerful interests. At a time when the press is focused on threats to democracy, climate change and public health crises, financial regulation is, to put it bluntly, hardly headline news. But a dozen years ago it was. And the news coverage of that period – which marked the most severe economic dislocation since the Great Depression – says much about the ability of elite news media to perform a watchdog role when the subject matter is complicated and ideologically charged.

The crisis prompted a raft of studies arguing news media had failed in their watchdog duties in the run-up to 2008. Multiple scholars characterised journalists as "cheerleaders" for the financial sector (Fraser 2009; Marron et al. 2010; Mohamed 2009; Stiglitz 2014). Matthew Fraser said this posture was one of the reasons journalists developed a condition he called "crash blindness." Maria Marron, Zeny Sarabia-Panol, Marianne Sison, Sandhya Rao and Ray Niekamp said the cheerleader label applied to generalists and business journalists alike. One longitudinal study, by Sophie Knowles, Gail Phillips and Johan Lidberg (2017), showed how news media appeared to abandon their watchdog role repeatedly during market booms. In analysing a recession in the early 1990s, the dot-com bubble and the 2008 crisis, the authors found a pattern of decreasing levels of forewarning and coverage regarding topics that were germane to the ensuring financial upheaval.

Some studies were focused inward, such as those which looked at newsroom skills and knowledge. Others were focused outward, such as those which considered journalist-source relations or commercial pressures. But before asking how and why journalists may have fallen short, there is the question as to whether those who cover finance even subscribe to a watchdog role. Damian Tambini interviewed journalists and discovered "considerable dispute regarding what constitutes responsible business and financial journalism" (Tambini 2008, p. 8).

Some saw themselves as having a mainly commercial role in terms of selling newspapers, others showed an awareness of the social function of financial journalism, and still others rejected the label of journalist altogether.

Nikki Usher (2013) suggested the question was not whether, but which – as in which version of a watchdog role journalists saw for themselves. Reporters at the *New York Times*, Usher noted, felt they had fulfilled their duties by following what she called the transmission model of the watchdog role. This is where journalists believe their job is to serve up information and let audiences decide what to make of it. But Usher also said audiences do not always listen. Chris Roush (2009) had made a similar point when he argued journalists *had* lived up to the watchdog role but were simply not heeded because audiences had been caught up in the bubble of a bull market. To Usher's critique, I would add that the transmission model may defang the journalist and empower other actors. Journalists could end up offering he-said-she-said journalism (Rosen 2009) or become influenced by external forces, such as those Herman and Chomsky listed in the propaganda model.

Fraser, Francesco Guerrera (2009), Danny Schechter (2009), Paula Chakravartty and Dan Schiller (2010) and Dean Starkman (2014), among others, investigated the reasons why few journalists asked probing questions about mortgage lending, risk-taking and the health of the banking industry. Among the factors they noted were a focus on access over accountability (Schechter 2009; Starkman 2014), and a lack of resourcing by profit-driven private media groups (Chakravartty and Schiller 2010; Schechter 2009). Mike Berry (2012) and Paul Manning (2013) focused on which sources news media gravitated towards, with the former noting a reliance during the crisis on private-sector economists at the expense of other voices, and the latter examining ways that mutually shared understandings discouraged journalists from being more critical. Another factor: journalists often did not possess the specialist knowledge needed to overcome the obfuscating effects of technical jargon (Fraser 2009). As Guerrera, who covered the crisis for the *Financial Times*, wrote: "We were lied to. We were not good enough or resourceful enough to see through the lies" (Guerrera 2009, p. 48).

But the question I am most interested in is less procedural and more ideological. Or rather, it is procedural in so far as ideology affects procedure. I wish to examine the paradigmatic assumptions that journalists and their sources made after the crisis. If journalists had been cheerleaders, a vital question is not just why they cheered, but whether they continued cheering afterwards. This book looks at a landmark U.S. law and how articles framed discussion in ways that embraced or rejected competing regulatory paradigms. It explores the degree to which elite journalists offered platforms for market liberal viewpoints and marginalised arguments favouring a paradigm shift. Ultimately, it aims to offer lessons applicable to news media more broadly in a post-pandemic era.

The procedural-ideological connection runs through the literature. Anya Schiffrin (2015) highlighted it when she pointed to research that showed how reliance on certain sources resulted in coverage that reflected neoliberal thinking. Keith Butterick (2015) argued that journalists had acted as cheerleaders for decades, as a growing PR industry and competitive pressures encouraged a passive posture that served corporate interests. Laura Basu (2018) showed how the financial crisis was repeatedly reframed in Britain to legitimise the policies that had led to the crisis.

What has been rarer, however, are quantitative studies on post-crisis media discourse according to ideological or paradigmatic orientation. Jesper Strömbäck, Toril Aalberg and Anders Jenssen (2010) did a comparative analysis of media behaviour and public attitudes about regulation in six countries in late 2008 and early 2009. That period, however, was while the crisis was still raging, and major regulatory initiatives had yet to take shape. It noted a tradition of hostility towards interventionism in the United States but did not see signs of that in either the content or public attitudes at that point. Thomas Bach, Mathias Weber and Oliver Quiring (2013) looked at framing in the German press, with several frame categories that had ideological dimensions (a self-regulation frame, a globalisation frame, etc.). But their study also focused on late 2008. Apart from that, there have been a handful of studies that offered quantitative framing analysis of post-crisis discourse in smaller countries such as Ireland (Cawley 2012), the Netherlands (Damstra and Vliegenthart 2018), Norway (Bjerke and Fonn 2015) and Sweden (Falasca 2014). A common theme in these works is the resilience of neoliberal ideas despite the crisis.

Having discussed literature on news media's watchdog role and their coverage of finance, the rest of this chapter provides context for the case studies that follow. The next section considers the relationship between a policy paradigm and ideology. I then trace the evolution of policy paradigms since the start of the 20th century. That brings us to the paradigmatic crossroads that journalists – and all of society – faced after 2008. Here, I discuss the Obama administration's response and public attitudes about regulation. This sets the scene for case studies of the narratives that emerged from the wreckage of 2008.

The grip of a policy paradigm

In "Eight Days," a fly-on-the-wall account in *The New Yorker* of efforts to save the investment bank Lehman Brothers in September 2008, James B. Stewart illustrated the grip a policy paradigm could hold over state decision-making. Stewart wrote of how Treasury Secretary Henry Paulson and others tried to orchestrate a private sector solution. As matters came to a head, Paulson "summoned Wall Street's chief executives to the Fed, where he said emphatically that there would be no government assistance, as had already been indicated to the press" (Stewart 2009). The episode underlined how constrained officials felt by the tenets of the prevailing market liberal paradigm. The journalist highlighted the moment in paradigmatic terms: "In an intellectual debate that has been going on since the Depression, Lehman's failure may mark a victory of John Maynard Keynes over Adam Smith – the government interventionists over laissez-faire capitalists" (Stewart 2009).

Lehman collapsed on 15 September 2008. The date, in the eyes of many economists, was a tipping point which pushed the world's financial system into its most severe crisis since the 1930s. The flow of institutional credit dried up; the value of assets plummeted; banks around the world failed or were threatened with bankruptcy; and governments led by the United States, Britain, Germany, Japan and China took aggressive measures to contain the crisis. The ensuing weeks led to a prolonged downturn. About that much, there appeared to be broad agreement. But in the years following Lehman, there was considerable dispute about what caused the crisis, and what policy choices made sense (Lo 2012). Meanwhile, the public, arguably for the first time in seven decades, was interested in financial regulation. Stefano Pagliari (2013) showed U.S. media coverage of financial regulation spiked to more than 0.4 percentage point of all measured articles in 2009–2010 from below 0.1 point in 2007 and below 0.05 point for much of the 1994–2007 period. Data for Britain showed a similar pattern.

Not long after Lehman's fall, a view took hold in the popular imagination that signs of the impending crisis had been there to be seen, if only people had looked carefully. In Britain, this notion was captured vividly in a newspaper account of a briefing given to Queen Elizabeth, whose own finances were hurt by the crisis. "Why did nobody notice it?" the Queen asked academics at the London School of Economics, perplexed that matters so large could occur without anyone paying attention (Pierce 2008). In the United States, the idea that tell-tale signs were hiding in plain sight provided the dramatic premise for Michael Lewis's book *The Big Short* (2010), which profiled several people who spotted them and profited spectacularly. Implicit in the comment from Queen Elizabeth and the storytelling of Lewis is the suggestion that some obstacle blocked people's vision. The obstacle for journalists, according to the cheerleader critique, was the market liberal paradigm.

Thomas Kuhn defined paradigms as "universally recognized scientific achievements that for a time provide model problems and solutions to a community of practitioners" (Kuhn 1970, p. viii). Kuhn was referring to paradigms that have emerged in the natural sciences, but numerous scholars in the social sciences have drawn on his theory. Peter Hall is one. Hall's influential 1993 study on an economic paradigm shift in Britain looked at the sociological process by which one school of thought came into the ascendency, including discussion of the role played by news media. He described policy paradigms as frameworks of ideas and standards that specified "not only the goals of policy and the kind of instruments that can be used to attain them, but also the very nature of the problems they are meant to be addressing" (Hall 1993, p. 279).[3] This is in line with Kuhn's view that paradigms compete to attract practitioners within a community. "Paradigms gain their status because they are more successful than their competitors in solving a few problems that the group of practitioners has come to recognize as acute" (Kuhn 1970, p. 23).

In the realm of financial policy, it would be easy to confuse the terms paradigm and ideology. In fact, Hall's description of a paradigm overlaps with the concept of an ideology as later defined by Michael Freeden (2003). Hall even conflates the terms, writing of how "two economic ideologies" (in this case Keynesianism and monetarism) were "distinct paradigms" (Hall 1993, p. 284). It's not hard to see why. Freeden, in describing the functions of a political ideology, says it is a set of ideas, beliefs, opinions and values that:

1 Exhibit a recurring pattern
2 Are held by significant groups
3 Compete over providing and controlling plans for public policy
4 Do so with the aim of justifying, contesting or changing the social and political arrangements and processes of a political community (Freeden 2003, p. 32).

This echoes Hall's conception of a paradigm, particularly with regards to plans for public policy.

It may be tempting, then, to use the terms interchangeably. In this analysis, however, I consider a paradigm as a *component* of an ideology, one that operates along the same principles of the ideology and may even help define those principles. This too fits with Freeden's analysis as he likens an ideology to a set of modular units of furniture which can be assembled in different ways. A policy paradigm supports an ideology through its explanatory or predictive power, while an ideology concerns a larger set of ideas, beliefs, opinions and values. Freeden's furniture-unit metaphor accounts for how both market liberal and interventionist paradigms can share some principles, such as the promotion of anti-trust measures (c.f. Shearmur 1997).

The evolution of policy paradigms

There appear to have been three loosely defined paradigms that dominated transatlantic policy thinking during the century leading to 2008. The first, which held sway until the Great Depression, we can call the laissez-faire paradigm. It argued that competition without state intervention was the basis for wealth (Aikins 2009). The second paradigm called for state policies that could combat the destabilising effects of market pressures and herd behaviour. Based on the ideas of Keynes, this paradigm dominated policy discussions from the mid-1930s to the 1970s (Chang 1997; Crouch 2009; Helleiner 1996). We can call this the interventionist policy paradigm. Finally, amid a series of economic shocks in the 1970s, a paradigm took root that argued for reduced intervention and renewed reliance on market competition (Chang 1997; Crouch 2009; Stiglitz 1993). We can call this third paradigm the market liberal paradigm.[4]

The Great Depression paved the way for the adoption of an interventionist paradigm. Timothy Canova (2009) notes that laissez-faire capitalism was still the prevailing orthodoxy in law and economics between the 1929 crash and the banking crisis of 1933. "Financial markets were largely unregulated and unsupervised, and it was not seen as the responsibility of government to stimulate economic activity, even in a recession" (Canova 2009, p. 371). The year 1933 was when Keynes published *The Means to Prosperity* as a policy remedy for the ills afflicting the developed world; his biographer, Robert Skidelsky (2003), wrote of how copies were sent to world leaders and taken seriously in Britain and the United States.

The acceptance of Keynes's ideas was exemplified by the New Deal of the Roosevelt administration. It was guided by a view that an unregulated free market would only perpetuate the dispossession the Great Depression had caused. Legal scholar Ioannis Glinavos wrote: "The Roosevelt administration responded to this popular perception by offering the countervailing power of government, administered by disinterested expert regulators, in order to discipline the market and stabilise an economy that laissez faire had all but destroyed" (Glinavos 2010, p. 4). Alan Blinder, a former central banker, describes one of the tenets underpinning Keynesianism as the notion that government can improve on the free market (Blinder 2008). Keynes called for fiscal policies to counterbalance boom and bust, treating state spending as a spigot that could run hot or cold. As an example of what Blinder would later write, Keynes argued:

> In conditions of laissez-faire the avoidance of wide fluctuations in employment may, therefore, prove impossible without a far-reaching change in the psychology of investment markets such as there is no reason to expect. I conclude that the duty of ordering the current volume of investment cannot safely be left in private hands. (Keynes 1936, p. 200)

Keynes was also focused on systemic risk. He called for down payment requirements for lending, including for corporate securities purchases (Canova 2009). His ideas later formed the basis of a hypothesis by Hyman Minsky (1992), which suggests capitalist economic systems can amplify economic movements. The Keynes-Minsky financial market theory featured in a number of post-2008 diagnoses (c.f. Crotty 2011; McCulley 2009; Sen 2010).

Among the more notable measures of this period was the Glass-Steagall Act of 1933, which required commercial banks and insurance companies to be kept separate from investment banking. This was in response to the view in Congress that banks had helped promote unsustainable booms in the real estate and securities markets (a view that would become prevalent again 75 years later). Another example of the paradigm's acceptance could be seen in the 1944 Bretton Woods summit, which Eric Helleiner called a constitution for the international financial system. Delegates sought to reconcile an open multilateral financial system with the more interventionist practices adopted after the Great Depression (Helleiner 1996). Ha-Joon Chang called the quarter-century after the Second World War the "age of regulation" as nations increasingly pursued activist economic policies (Chang 1997, p. 704).

Keynesian interventionism held sway into the 1970s, but a process of paradigm contestation had begun more than two decades earlier. In 1947, a group of thinkers led by the economist Friedrich Hayek and including fellow economist Milton Friedman formed the Mont Pèlerin

Society. Although a history of the society says the group had no official views or policies (Butler n.d.), many of its members rejected the idea of interventionism and called for a new type of liberal economic and financial policymaking approach.

The market liberal paradigm that evolved from their ideas has at times been equated – in scholarship and the media – with laissez-faire capitalism. But the society's founders were neither primarily libertarian nor intractably anti-regulatory. A statement of aims issued after the society's initial meeting mooted the "possibility of establishing minimum standards by means not inimical to initiative and function of the market" (The Mont Pèlerin Society 2020). This mirrored an observation by Hayek, who wrote in *The Road to Serfdom* (1944) of how competition did not preclude some types of government interference as long as it was aimed at boosting competition. "Planning and competition can be combined only by planning for competition, not by planning against competition" (Hayek 1944, p. 46).

This third paradigm called for limiting regulation to that which reinforced the integrity of the market and market mechanisms (Peck 2008). Concurrent with an oil price shock and an international debt crisis in the 1970s, the ideas of Hayek and Friedman gained traction as their fame began to spread beyond the narrow world of economics. Hayek won the Nobel prize for economics in 1974 and Friedman won it in 1976. They both advocated an anti-statist system which designated the market as the guarantor of individual freedom. Matt Guardino and Dean Snyder wrote: "Although the neoliberals were marginalized in elite policy circles through the 1950s and 1960s, the economic crises of the 1970s opened a window for their ascendance" (Guardino and Snyder 2012, p. 528).

Efforts to take advantage of that window can be seen in a public campaign by Friedman. He launched a book and 10-part television series called *Free to Choose* (1980). In the tradition of Keynes himself, Friedman had become a public intellectual. He had been contributing articles to *Newsweek*, the *Wall Street Journal* and the *New York Times* since the 1960s. By becoming a television figure, Friedman widened his audience further. In an interview to promote the series, Friedman explained:

> ... I feel so strongly that America is at a critical point in its history. For the past 50 years, we have been moving away from the fundamental principles that made this great country, the fundamental principles of freedom – economic, political – of relying on the individual, of keeping government in its place, of keeping government to be as an umpire. (Free to Choose Network 2012)

According to a not-for-profit organisation devoted to advancing Friedman's ideas, nearly 20 million Americans watched at least part of the series (Free to Choose Network 2012). In the 1980s, neoliberalism and the market liberal paradigm were championed by U.S. President Ronald Reagan and British Prime Minister Margaret Thatcher. They deregulated business, privatised public services, slashed taxes and institutionalised a global free trade regime (Guardino and Snyder 2012). Reagan, in his first inaugural address, spoke of the economic malaise of the day and famously said: "In this present crisis, government is not the solution to our problem, government is the problem" (Reagan 1981). Free market competition, shareholder value and liberalised capital flows became the priorities (Borio and White 2003; Canova 2009; Crouch 2009; Glinavos 2010; Guardino and Snyder 2012). This ideological viewpoint, Guardino and Snyder said, would define U.S. political economy for the next 30-plus years.

The 2008 crisis: 'A state of shocked disbelief'

Just as major crises in the 1930s and 1970s called into question aspects of the then-dominant regulatory paradigms, the 2008 crisis challenged a key tenet of the market liberal paradigm. Kuhn argues that a precondition for a paradigm shift is that there is an anomaly that cannot be explained by the current dominant paradigm. The undermining of a central tenet of market liberalism can thus be seen, in Kuhnian terms, as an unexplained anomaly. The tenet here was the view that the market, underpinned by self-interest, could be self-regulating.

Former Federal Reserve Chairman Alan Greenspan had long been one of the most forceful advocates of market liberalism in his dealings with politicians, regulatory officials and the press. On 23 October 2008, at the height of the crisis, he said self-regulation had failed. "Those of us who have looked to the self-interest of lending institutions to protect shareholders' equity, myself included, are in a state of shocked disbelief," Greenspan told a Congressional panel (Andrews 2008). Greenspan had been lionised in the media, the political sphere and regulatory circles since his appointment as governor of the Federal Reserve in 1987. Here, a *New York Times* article described him as "humbled" (Andrews 2008).

In charting the evolution of paradigms, scholars have identified a sine curve trend, as regulatory approaches shift back and forth between looser and stricter oversight (Coffee 2013). The economic historian Karl Polanyi described a similar pattern that he called a "double movement," where the ideas shaping society were pushing either towards or against laissez-faire. In *The Great Transformation* (1957), Polanyi considered the notion of self-regulation within a market economy in opposition to the interventionist idea that state action was needed to steer the market.[5] The prospect of a shift in the sine curve towards interventionism appeared to be at hand after the 2008 U.S. general election. In November 2008, President-elect Barack Obama's choice for chief of staff, Rahm Emanuel, paraphrased Winston Churchill when he said: "You never want a serious crisis to go to waste, and what I mean by that is an opportunity to do things that you think you could not do before" (Wall Street Journal CEO Council 2008).

Resistance to a shift towards more stringent oversight, however, soon emerged. Glinavos wrote of how the private sector persuaded governments from abandoning "the market liberalising imperatives of the last two decades" (Glinavos 2010, p. 10). He cited the avoidance of nationalisation despite the massive bailouts that financial firms required. This is not to say that bank nationalisation is some kind of litmus test of paradigmatic change. Roosevelt also had resisted the temptation to nationalise banks, while still introducing measures that became emblematic of the interventionist paradigm (Schlesinger 1958).

The Obama administration responded with an omnibus regulatory law, one shepherded by Senate Banking Committee Chairman Christopher Dodd and House Financial Services Committee Chairman Barney Frank. In July 2010, after more than a year of legislative wrangling, the Dodd-Frank Wall Street Reform and Consumer Protection Act became law (111th Congress 2010). "The Act is widely described as the most ambitious and far-reaching overhaul of financial regulation since the 1930s" (Acharya et al. 2010, p. 1). Proponents framed it as an effort to introduce order to an out-of-control marketplace. Critics argued that it was intrusive and overly burdensome, that it failed to address the causes of the crisis, and that it would lead to economic malaise.

By almost any measure, Dodd-Frank was a more interventionist initiative than any U.S. regulatory development in decades. Its scope was far broader than the Savings and Loans regulation of 1989 or the Sarbanes-Oxley Act on corporate governance in 2002. Dodd-Frank targeted major institutions that operated in global markets and retail-oriented firms that dealt with the public. It created a body for overseeing financial and non-financial institutions, consolidated regulatory agencies, introduced a bureau to provide consumer protections and created tools that would allow the government to wind down firms posing a systemic threat.

The size of Dodd-Frank (some 2,300 pages) and the number of rules it produced (more than 400) testified to its breadth. It was more than 60 times as large as the 37-page Glass-Steagall Act. Dodd said markets were far more complex than anything Senator Carter Glass and Representative Henry B. Steagall had faced (Dodd 2010). But Republican lawmakers such as Spencer Bachus and Jeb Hensarling, who succeeded Frank as the next two chairmen of the House Financial Services Committee, weaponised the law's page length as a symbol of regulatory overreach, repeatedly referring to it in statements and hearings. A Nexis search based on their names, the figure "2,300" and the term "Dodd-Frank" between July 2010 and June 2018 showed 220 occasions where those terms were linked together.[6]

The shock that Greenspan described had been felt virtually everywhere. Yet, despite the scale of the upheaval, the resistance to a paradigm shift proved effective. This can be seen in public opinion polling data and a surge in anti-statist sentiment. A paradigm shift, as we have considered it, requires not only changes in official policy but also a sense of consensus in favour of the new approach. Initially, the public's views about Dodd-Frank ranged from lukewarm to positive. But as the shock from the crisis wore off, people reverted to pre-crisis stances, seeing regulation more as a drag on the economy than a guardrail.[7]

In a recurring survey, Pew Research Center asked whether government regulation of business was needed to protect the public or would do more harm than good. In October 2008, 50% said it was necessary and 38% thought it would do more harm than good; by February 2012, the numbers had reversed, as 40% deemed it necessary while 52% saw it doing more harm than good (Pew Research Center 2012). Gallup surveys pointed to an even stronger vein of anti-regulatory sentiment. The data suggest the U.S. public appeared to have had deep-seated feelings about regulation which only temporarily were influenced by crisis hardship.

Figure 1.1 shows worries about too much regulation growing substantially just before and after the passage of Dodd-Frank (Gallup 2020).

Agenda-building and news media narratives

The evolution of policy paradigms and evidence of shifting public opinion offer context for the book's central question about news media behaviour during a period of re-regulation. When salience about an issue increases dramatically, as it did in the case of financial regulation, news media form a key part of an agenda-building process. Charles Elder and Roger Cobb describe agenda-building as "the process through which

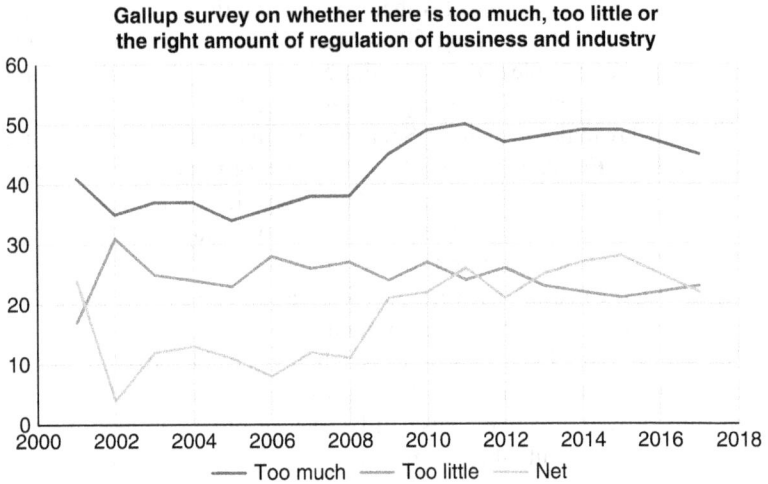

Gallup survey on whether there is too much, too little or the right amount of regulation of business and industry

Figure 1.1 Time series of Gallup survey on regulation.

problems or issues come to command the active and serious attention of government as prospective matters of public policy" (Elder and Cobb 1984, p. 115). The importance of agenda-building arises from two facts, they say. One is that there are always more matters vying for government attention than can be considered. Another is that policy problems are not givens but are matters of definition. In both cases, news media are central. The press is often the route by which issues come to command the government's attention or get defined, primarily via the media's own agenda-setting function (Berkowitz 1992; McCombs 2005; McCombs and Shaw 1972; Rogers and Dearing 1988).

The scope for news media to create, reinforce or counter narratives takes on extra significance because those narratives can form a link between broader ideological concerns and the narrower policy changes that coalitions wish to pursue. Researchers such as Mark McBeth, Elizabeth Shanahan, Ruth Arnell and Paul Hathaway (2007) and Deborah Stone (2002) have explored the ways that actors build narratives. In fact, McBeth, Robert Tokle and Susan Schaefer (2018) showed how post-crisis economic coverage (in this case by broadcasters) prioritised narrative concerns over empirical evidence. Their study – like many others in the narrative policy analysis arena – was based on a framework which defined a policy narrative as having at least one character. This could be a villain (who causes a problem) or a victim (who is harmed by the problem) or a hero (who identifies and/or fixes a problem). This framework bears a strong resemblance to the framing taxonomy developed by Robert Entman (1993), which categorised news frames into four types: problems, causes, solutions and moral judgments. I will develop this idea in Chapter 2. The framing of issues, either by elite text journalists or their sources, formed the basis of an over-arching post-crisis narrative that undermined the role of the state in overseeing markets. The research here does not offer a normative argument in favour of an interventionist paradigm. Rather, it focuses on how ideas can infuse coverage and favour one paradigm over another. The analysis is based on nearly three years of coverage in the *New York Times* and *Washington Post*, and interviews with journalists who reported on the regulatory story for major national and international news providers.

Notes

1 Litan said he had shelved plans for a book about evidence-based policy-making. "No one wanted to listen to experts on anything, whether it's climate change or vaccines," he told me. "I think the crisis had an enormous amount to do with that."
2 The concern from McChesney and Nichols was shared by Jürgen Habermas, who saw the PR industry as particularly corrosive. In PR, a message sender "hides his business intentions" as someone interested in public welfare (Habermas 1991, p. 193).
3 Mattei Dogan (1996) argues a paradigm occurs "only when one testable theory alone dominates all other theories and is accepted by the entire scientific community," which he says does not occur in social sciences (Dogan 1996, p. 299). This view is not shared by many in other fields (c.f. Pearce 1995). Kuhn himself was inspired by contact with social scientists as he was struck by their disagreements about the legitimacy of problems and methods. He concluded that scientific progress was not different in kind from progress in other fields, but that natural sciences typically were not marked by competing views on aims and standards, making progress in a natural science community easier to see.
4 This third paradigm has been referred to as neoliberalism, although here I view neoliberalism as an ideology rather than a paradigm in that it concerns a wider set of concerns than regulatory problems. Economists such as Joseph Stiglitz and Paul Krugman have pejoratively used the term "market fundamentalism." To avoid being normative, I have not used this term.
5 The sociologist Fred Block wrote of Polanyi's hopes that a durable paradigm, based on interventionist principles, might emerge. Block says the question remains open as to whether humanity is "doomed to endless cycles in which one movement is in the ascendancy followed by the other" (Block 2008).
6 Under Hensarling, the Congressional committee's website as of June 2018 included a section called "The Failures of Dodd-Frank." It noted the page

figure, said the act enshrined the notion of financial firms being "too big to fail" and argued that rising banking fees were due to the law. In 2018, Democrats took control of the House of Representatives and the committee's website was redesigned, omitting those references.

7 From Walter Lippmann to John Dewey to Pierre Bourdieu, thinkers have found the notion of public opinion problematic. A specific worry concerns polling data due to the way questions may be presented (Bishop 2004; Splichal 1999). Nonetheless, to the extent that paradigm shift is sociological, the public mood matters and such data offer a means to glean it.

2 Market liberalism on display: Regulatory coverage before the crisis

By a range of measures, the *New York Times* and *Washington Post* set the pace for news coverage of government affairs in the United States. Whether one considers citations by other media, Pulitzer Prize tallies, circulation figures or anecdotal evidence from the policy community, these newspapers are among the top publications in the country. Their scope for intermedia agenda setting may have been dented slightly by the proliferation of new political voices in the Internet era, but researchers say they have continued to wield considerable influence (Farnsworth and Lichter 2005; Meraz 2009). The impact of their choices in terms of topics, sources, language and issues thus extends far beyond their direct readership.

This level of influence effectively guaranteed the *Post* and the *Times* a role in the paradigm contestation that took place after the crisis. Did journalists at these newspapers adjust their approaches to covering regulatory news, factoring in the paradigmatic implications of the upheaval? Did they view either the financial industry or the policy community as particularly blameworthy and see it as their journalistic duty to explore how and why? In short, was there any indication they embraced the idea of a policy paradigm shift? Or instead, did they – and other elite media – view the crisis like other big stories, as something requiring attention but not much soul-searching on their own part?

To answer such questions, we need to consider how elite media performed both before and after the crisis. This is not straightforward because the collective attitudes of journalists are generally not on full display. American journalism for decades has emphasised neutrality and, to the extent it is possible, objectivity (Cunningham 2003; Schudson 2001; Skovsgaard et al. 2013). It is a tradition celebrated at both newspapers, so anyone looking for patterns that showed systemic bias in favour of a paradigm would be unlikely to find it from explicit language within the news section of either publication.

DOI: 10.4324/9781003177944-2

Framing theory offers a way to approach the task. By examining news texts in detail to identify patterns in the way issues are framed, we can start to see the paradigmatic assumptions built into the coverage. This chapter will outline a method for quantitative analysis of news framing and use it to consider a major regulatory story from nearly a decade before the crisis: the repeal of the Glass-Steagall Act. The legislation came at a time when policymakers – and much of society – were in thrall to a market liberal paradigm.

Identifying narratives

We can think of media analysis in terms of three interrelated and sometimes overlapping categories: (1) media production, (2) media content and (3) media effects. The first category refers to factors that influence media behaviour, such as external pressures that may affect journalists in their choices of subjects, sources or language. The second is focused on understanding the nature of journalistic output, which could come from qualitative or quantitative content analysis or discourse analysis of texts. The third category concerns the effects news coverage may have on the public or specific actor groups. In the case of financial policy, that would be not only regulators and policy experts but also politicians and the voters who elect those politicians.

These categories can blur together, and in that sense, one could use a Venn diagram to visualise them. In line with work by Stuart Hall (Hall, S. 1973), I find it helpful to think in terms of their causal relationships and the way that media effects may influence media production as part of a feedback loop (Figure 2.1). The research presented here does not extend to media effects, which has long been a fraught subject in journalism studies and has only become more complicated

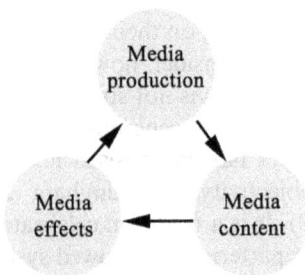

Figure 2.1 Media feedback loop.

due to the advent of social media. Rather, the analysis focuses on media content and media production.

Chapter 1 discussed the idea that narratives could be used to build support for policy positions and ultimately for a paradigm. Narratives may derive their persuasive power from rhetorical devices, or they may be considered rhetorical devices themselves. They are often appeals to people's emotions. But we also know that news reporters tend to eschew using rhetoric themselves. Their stated aim is to report news, not win debates. Could news media coverage establish narratives via other, non-rhetorical means?

First, we should define our terms. One way to think of a news narrative is as a collective description of a series of events. Heroes, villains and victims are depicted based on that sequence of events and the authors will connect the dots. Another way to think of a narrative is as a theme in news coverage. This could involve the repetition of certain ideas or concepts, such as the pros and cons of market liberalism or interventionism. If the ideas or concepts are repeated often enough, we may speak of a media narrative that focuses on them. They still may tell a story by pointing to heroes, villains and victims, only in this case the audience is left to connect the dots. This is broadly how two authors from the Brookings Institution, Martin Baily and Douglas Elliott, use the term in their paper "Telling the narrative of the financial crisis: Not just a housing bubble" (2009) (Chapter 3). Finally, there is the notion of a media narrative based on relationships and causality. In that sense, it is similar to the way we think about paradigms and ideologies. Here we may speak of a media narrative as a set of ideas about relationships that emerge in a text, based on a particular view of how the world works. For instance, a media narrative that promotes interventionism may be one that validates it by endorsing or repeatedly referencing the tenets of an interventionist paradigm. This last description is akin to what Roland Barthes conceived of as myth (Barthes 1957).

Since media narratives typically depend on repetition, a quantitative approach to analysing them makes sense. Quantitative analysis of the ideological dimension of discourse has been pursued in numerous strands of research, such as studies that seek to make claims about media bias (Covert and Wasburn 2007; Groseclose and Milyo 2005) or those that aim to establish empirical linguistic evidence of ideological currents that run through large volumes of political texts (López and Llopis 2010; Sim et al. 2013). Some of these studies take advantage of extraneous data to provide an ideological scale against which evidence of the discourse can be indexed, as in the case of a study by Tim Groseclose and Jeffrey Milyo.

Others rely on automated linguistic analysis (c.f. Sim et al. 2013; López and Llopis 2010). What matters in all cases is the unit of analysis. For this research, the unit is the media frame.

Actors building an agenda that promotes a policy or policy paradigm can be expected to use whatever methods will help them to succeed. One method that has received extensive academic attention is framing. The concept of media framing is often traced to Erving Goffman, who referred to individuals' attempts to "locate, perceive, identify and label" issues via "schemata of interpretation" (Goffman 1974, p. 21). Media theorists have offered a variety of definitions, although most focus on the idea that a frame creates perspective, salience or organising qualities (Entman 1993; Gamson and Modigliani 1987, 1989; McCombs 2005; Scheufele 1999; Tankard et al. 1991). Among the researchers who have contributed to framing theory, two stand out for the purpose of considering agenda-building and paradigm contestation: Robert Entman and Max McCombs.

Entman provided a basic framing taxonomy. He wrote:

> Framing essentially involves selection and salience. To frame is to select some aspects of a perceived reality and make them more salient in a communicating text, in such a way as to promote a particular problem definition, causal interpretation, moral evaluation, and/or treatment recommendation for the item described. (Entman 1993, p. 52)[1]

From a quantitative perspective, the use of frame categories allows one to analyse their usage for patterns. Entman's subsequent framing model, based on the concept of "cascading activation" (Entman 2003, p. 417), offered a tool for understanding the power of framing beyond the traditional unidirectional conception (media to audience).[2] He suggested frames offered by elites not only can be passed on via the media to the public but also that they may be sent back "upwards" and have fresh effects on state elites; similarly, frames generated by the public may have effects on the media (Entman 2003, p. 419). The scope for multidirectional movement by frames allows their messages to be amplified.[3]

McCombs has considered framing within the parameters of the agenda-setting theory he co-developed, which was based on a correlation coefficient between what people saw as important issues and what got reported. He labelled the subjects that appeared in news reports (people, issues, events, etc.) as "objects" and said those objects in turn had attributes. For McCombs, a frame is an attribute of an object because it describes the object. The media's choices of objects (e.g., crime, the economy, etc.) constitute first-level agenda setting, while the choices of attributes represent second-level agenda setting. Both Entman and McCombs thus offer framing theories that allow for not only qualitative but also quantitative analysis.

Agenda-setting theory was based on a much-cited observation by Bernard Cohen: "The press may not be successful much of the time in telling people what to think, but it is stunningly successful in telling its readers what to think about" (Cohen 1963, p. 13). First-level agenda-setting studies have borne out the "what to think about" part of the comment. But the idea of second-level agenda setting opens the door to telling people "what to think."[4] Also, from an agenda-building perspective, we should remember that frames are not generated solely by journalists. Actors such as state officials or special interest representatives also may frame issues (Brüggemann 2014), provided they can make their way into the news pages.

News media thus may establish or support narratives not through the force of evidence, logic or explicitly rhetorical language (as a policy champion might), but through repetition of ideas and perspectives.[5] The narratives that emerge in turn can promote or support a paradigm, which itself may promote or support an ideology, as illustrated in Figure 2.2. Underpinning this approach is the belief that the weight attached to different types of utterances matters. In the context of paradigmatic discourse, that requires an understanding of the nature of the utterances, including the authors, texts, chronology and frequency. Quantitative analysis can also provide clues about production. In identifying the weight that is attached to different voices, concepts, issues, etc., we can identify aspects of the news coverage worthy of closer

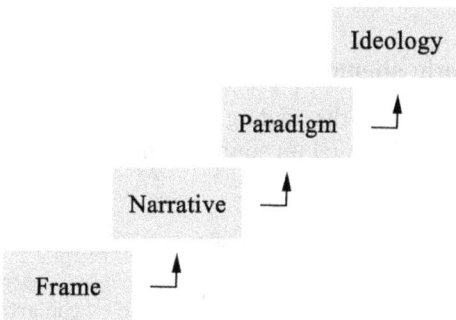

Ideology

Paradigm

Narrative

Frame

Figure 2.2 News framing and narratives: A conceptual framework.

inspection from a production perspective so as to understand why those voices, concepts, issues, etc. may have appeared so frequently, or so rarely, in the texts. M. Mark Miller and Bonnie Parnell Riechert (2001) argue for the importance of frame frequency, noting the ways that actors seek to gain support for their positions by offering new facts or altering the interpretive dimensions by which facts are to be evaluated.

The task, then, is to identify a way to view frames and see how they collectively support narratives. We can begin by thinking in terms of frame types. Entman's four types – problems, causes, solutions and moral judgments – offer a starting point. For this research, two categories were added based on analysis by Claes de Vreese, Jochen Peter and Holli Semetko (2001). Citing various U.S. studies, they suggest that "news about politics and the economy is often framed in terms of conflict or in terms of the economic consequences of events, issues, and policies" (de Vreese, Peter and Semetko 2001, p. 109). The resulting six-frame taxonomy – made up of Entman's four types plus conflict and consequences – can consider discourse about policy paradigms.

To understand narratives in these leading newspapers, I looked at their coverage of regulatory reform between 2009 and 2012,[6] identifying the ways that ideas, people, events or issues were framed on a sentence-by-sentence basis. I categorised these frames based on where they appeared in the news story (priority), who offered them (source), the type of frame employed (from the six categories) and what kind of paradigm they aligned with, if any.[7]

The Dodd-Frank bill was unveiled in June 2009, so the sample period began on 1 June 2009. It ran to 31 March 2012, into the early phase of the 2012 presidential election. In between those two dates were the mid-term elections of 2010, the conclusion and release of a major Congressional investigation into the causes of the financial crisis, and the beginning of the implementation phase of Dodd-Frank.[8]

Determining paradigmatic alignment

The six-frame taxonomy made the coding of framing by type a straightforward affair. To code based on source, I chose the following categories:

1 State actors (with politicians and unelected officials as sub-categories)
2 News media (instances where the framing was done by the article's author or authors)

3 Corporate actors (with representatives of both financial and non-financial companies or their agents as sub-categories)
4 Independent elites (think tanks, academics and prominent commentators)
5 Advocacy groups
6 The public (e.g., vox pop)

Coding to determine paradigmatic alignment, however, required more judgment. Chapter 1, in charting the evolution of regulatory paradigms, referred to a sine curve phenomenon as the orientation of the dominant paradigm shifted between the state and the market. This suggests there are two opposing poles towards which successive paradigms are oriented, one based on prioritising market competition and the other on prioritising state objectives. Arguments for paradigms that are oriented in either direction are based on economic principles that economists and other policy advocates hold, and these principles form the tenets of the paradigms.

The use of two broadly defined generic paradigms (market liberal and interventionist) is reductionist in that it does not represent specific historical paradigms in their nuance and complexity (consider terms such as neo-Keynesian, post-Keynesian, etc.). But it has the benefit of allowing one to classify texts in terms of their alignment with either paradigm category based on sets of underlying principles, and in so doing lends itself to a quantitative method. To illustrate this concept, Table 2.1 gives an idea of how a series of different policy aims can be categorised as aligned with one generic paradigm or the other.[9]

The terms "market liberalism" and "interventionism" may be misleading because both paradigms embrace free-market capitalism. There is no question, for instance, that Keynes believed in many of Adam Smith's ideas and that Keynes advocated a version of economic liberalism. But a market liberal paradigm, as the term is used here, prioritises market competition over other concerns; an interventionist paradigm does not automatically give market competition the same primacy.

The notion of a paradigmatic sine curve does not provide clues about the length of the intervals between changes in direction, or the factors that may result in changes. Furthermore, there are no standard measures for when consensus has been reached and shift has occurred. For the natural sciences, Kuhn referred to practitioners being attracted to a new paradigm because it was better at solving problems. The "practitioners" in the case of a regulatory paradigm in a high-salience environment go beyond the regulators who help formulate and implement policy; they include the politicians who agree policy legislation, private

Table 2.1 Examples of links between policy prescriptions and paradigms

Policy aims	Paradigm	Rationale based on economic principles
Unimpeded supply/ demand process for the value of labour or capital	Market liberal	Markets are designed to maximise value and they perform this role best when there are fewer impediments.
Progressive tax policy	Interventionist	The state can improve on free markets by allocating resources to areas that markets are not equipped to address, areas which, if developed, will benefit the wider economy.
Prudential standards for capital adequacy	Interventionist	Individual banks may be susceptible to a short-term focus on profit and may not be able to self-determine safe capital adequacy levels, creating systemic risk.
Full private sector discretion concerning remuneration practices	Market liberal	Unhindered competition for labour in the private sector will result in the best ideas surfacing, leading to greater innovation.

sector actors who will be subject to regulation and seek to influence it, and researchers who provide input and expertise during the policy-making process. Any measure that indicates consensus, ideally, would take all or at least most of these actor groups into account. When Milton Friedman famously said, "We are all Keynesians now" in 1965 (*Time* 1965), it was 20 years after the end of World War II, when interventionism was already dominating policy. Determining paradigm shift thus is not something that occurs in real time.

To consider whether news frames were in alignment with one paradigm or another, I created a thumbnail description of each generic paradigm, which could act as a reference text when coding news articles.

Market liberal paradigm narrative
A market liberal paradigm sees the market as best equipped to determine value. It does this through constant self-correction, a property made possible because markets' verdicts reflect more

information than those made by individuals. The paradigm holds that the state may misdiagnose problems and their causes due to incomplete information, potentially resulting in unforeseen consequences from state-designed solutions. It argues that allowing markets to dictate policy solutions is safer and fairer than allowing the state to. It calls for regulation to be limited to that which bolsters the integrity of the market. Any other restrictions may hinder the market from performing its value-determination function.

Interventionist paradigm narrative
An interventionist paradigm questions the ability of the market to consistently self-correct in a timely fashion, leading to states of boom and bust. It holds that short-termism and herd mentality, if left unchecked, can lead to problems. The paradigm views some societal needs as best suited to collective action by the state because market mechanisms are unsuitable or potentially unfair. An interventionist paradigm may rely on market mechanisms for some tasks, but it calls for safeguards since information gaps may hinder the market's ability to identify emerging risks. It argues that the cost of regulation is outweighed by the potential consequences of inaction. An additional moral justification is that the benefits of inaction would be enjoyed by a small group, while the negative consequences of inaction could be felt widely.

Each description refers to problems, causes, solutions, moral judgments and consequences; there is conflict in the way that each paradigm is presented in opposition to other views in the marketplace of ideas. The descriptions treat the state, the market and the public as potential heroes, villains or victims, in line with a narrative policy framework developed by Michael Jones and Mark McBeth (2010), which has been regularly used in narrative policy analysis literature since its introduction.

This research involved nearly 2,000 instances of frame coding. That includes frame types (problems, causes, consequences, etc.) as well as "sub-frames," where the types of problems, causes or consequences were categorised. In some cases, such as when a frame is offered by an actor other than the journalist, the paradigmatic alignment may be explicit. In other cases, identifying alignment may be implicit and require logical leaps. In many other cases, a frame simply may not indicate alignment with any paradigm, or it may be too ambiguous to tell.

A simple count of the total number of frames supporting an interventionist paradigm would suggest that the market liberal paradigm was in full retreat after the financial crisis. That would fit with the idea that elite news media are inherently more left-leaning and naturally would be biased in favour of a paradigm shift towards interventionism. But that would be misleading for a structural reason. The biggest category of frames in the sample were solution frames; most of these were coded as aligned with an interventionist paradigm simply because they were referring to Dodd-Frank (an interventionist measure) being proposed as a solution. This had the effect of skewing the data totals. As the rest of the book will show, different types of frames displayed different patterns. Ultimately, the project's conceptual framework, which positions frames in terms of narratives, paradigms and ideologies, offers a means of systematically understanding the ways that framing can be understood in terms of bias, as proposed by Entman (2007).

Pre-crisis regulatory coverage: A market liberal perspective

The analysis begins with a review of coverage from a time when the market liberal paradigm was largely undisputed. The Gramm-Leach-Bliley Act of 1999 repealed key parts of the Banking Act of 1933, more commonly known as the Glass-Steagall Act. This was a long-sought-after goal for large banks (Hendrickson 2001). It was also a goal for those who championed market liberalism, such as Federal Reserve Governor Alan Greenspan. The market liberal paradigm advocated deregulation wherever possible. It saw the "invisible hand" of the market as the best way to determine value thanks to the marketplace's capacity for absorbing and aggregating information. To the extent that news media reflects or plays a role in paradigm contestation, we should therefore expect to see evidence of an embrace of market liberalism in news coverage of pre-crisis regulatory matters.

Six months of articles in the *New York Times* and the *Washington Post* were analysed: five months leading up to the new law and one month that followed.[10] This produced 19 items in the *Times* and seven items in the *Post*. Of these, four *New York Times* articles contained only a passing reference to Glass-Steagall and featured no text about policy; as a result, they were omitted from the sample. Of the remaining 15, there were 11 news stories, two market reports, an editorial and a news round-up digest. The *Washington Post* sample featured five news items and two op-ed pieces. The amount of regulatory news coverage in this period was dwarfed by what occurred after 2008, but it nonetheless shows that the story received attention. What the sample lacks in size it makes up for in consistency. Articles routinely framed Glass-Steagall regulations as overly restrictive and outdated. They touted the benefits of deregulation, advancing a narrative that was clearly aligned with a market liberal paradigm.[11]

Gramm-Leach-Bliley was enacted on 12 November 1999. The law widened the range of activities banking companies could conduct, allowing single holding companies to offer banking, securities and insurance, in line with pre-Depression policy (Barth, Brumbaugh and Wilcox 2000). It was the culmination of years of efforts to repeal Glass-Steagall (Hendrickson 2001; John 1999). Despite a growing consensus throughout the 1980s and into the 1990s that deregulation offered economic benefits, there was opposition from pockets of the private sector (Hendrickson 2001). Small banks opposed reform for fear that it would allow large banks to run them out of business. Security firms, on the other hand, wanted to expand into commercial banking and favoured reform. Insurance firms were concerned about the prospect of competition from commercial banks. The insurance sector was won over by provisions that would restrict bank-holding companies to selling insurance products only in home states. By the end, only opposition from small banks remained and this was not enough to derail the legislation (Hendrickson 2001).[12]

A narrative emerges

In narrative terms, this coverage portrayed the banking industry as an economic hero, one aided by most state actors but opposed by special interests or politicians who lacked the wisdom to see the benefits of deregulation. The narrative paints restrictions on bank activity as a problem, one whose cause is outdated thinking. The solution is sweeping deregulation, which is needed to clear away the barriers to progress that resulted from old-fashioned notions; in fact, a broom metaphor recurs in the texts. The broom of deregulation will bring prosperity, this narrative argues; and if politicians are too timid to enact reforms, economic damage will result. The sample consistently framed Glass-Steagall as a problem, one whose consequences were high costs. It characterised old regulation as no longer suitable for the modern world. Gramm-Leach-Bliley was thus framed as a solution that would result in more economic prosperity.

In framing Glass-Steagall's restrictions as a problem, articles frequently alluded to the cause (the law) but in a way that minimised references to the legislation's original rationale. Instead, they depicted Glass-Steagall as crafted for another time. The terms "Depression" or

"Depression-era" featured 17 times in the *Times* sample and six times in the *Post* sample. The implied message: the world had moved on.

In a 1 July 1999 article on the start of debate over the bill to replace Glass-Steagall, the *Times* referred to the old law as "legislation rooted in the nightmarish experiences of the Depression" (Labaton 1999a). The article quotes an insurance industry association official saying: "It's because the market has advanced to such a degree that everyone has decided it's in their interests to have this bill." The next day, when the House of Representatives voted overwhelmingly in favour of the bill, the *Times* led its article by referring to the prospective removal of the last "remnants" of regulation from this earlier era (Labaton 1999b). At the *Post*, a change in the law was described as inevitable because of "decades of economic change that had made the old rules outdated" (Day 1999a).

The newspapers' framing focused on solutions as well as problems and their causes. In an article on 12 October, the *Times* wrote of legislation that would "tear down the Depression-era barriers" (Labaton 1999c), presenting the solution frame in approving terms and using the more negative problem frame of "barriers." The barrier reference was included again three days later, with an important extra element. On 15 October 1999, the *Times* referred to "the repeal of the Glass-Steagall Act of 1933 and other barriers to competition" (Labaton 1999d). To see how this framing Glass-Steagall as a problem aligns with a market liberal paradigm, one can consider the notion of capitalism's creative destruction that the economist Joseph Schumpeter (1942) had described.

When cause frames did refer to the original rationale for separating commercial and investment banking activity, it was done in vague terms. There were two exceptions to this. The *Times* article on the passage of Gramm-Leach Bliley contained four paragraphs (within a 32-paragraph article) that focused on systemic risk and featured the views of those warning of dangers (consequence frames) from undoing the regulations. A second exception came in a *Post* article days before the law's passage. It referenced two systemic risk-based rationales for Glass-Steagall, one concerning the sale of securities and the other concerning interest rate competition for savings products (Day 1999b). But the *Post* article added that economists no longer believed the two practices in question had caused the 1929 crash or the Great Depression, suggesting that Glass-Steagall itself had been built partly on false assumptions.

The frame type that appeared most strikingly in coverage was the consequence frame. It was mostly used to depict the economic benefit from unleashing the potential of banks, or conversely the economic cost from not doing so. In the 1 July 1999 article, the *Times* wrote of the "sweeping deregulation that would make it easier for banks, insurers and securities companies to enter each other's businesses" (Labaton 1999a).

A *Times* article on 2 July 1999 article on the House approval noted how Glass-Steagall could make it "prohibitively expensive" for affiliations between investment banks, commercial banks and insurers (Labaton 1999b). The *Post's* coverage on 31 October 1999 reported on lobbyists selling the bill's benefits in terms of creating jobs, increasing competition and helping consumers; it also highlighted Treasury officials' view that the legislation would make the industry more efficient and save it an estimated $15 billion a year (Day 1999b). When Gramm-Leach-Bliley was approved on 5 November 1999, the *Times* lead focused on the benefits that a less restrictive policy would bring:

> Congress approved landmark legislation today that opens the door for a new era on Wall Street in which commercial banks, securities houses and insurers will find it easier and cheaper to enter one another's businesses. (Labaton 1999e)

The article quoted the Treasury Secretary saying American companies would be better equipped to compete in the new economy.

Often the frames were used in conjunction with each other, such as in a 24 October 1999 op-ed piece in the *New York Times*. In endorsing the proposed law, the *Times* wrote:

> Legislation agreed to by the White House and the Republican leadership will sweep away the Depression-era curbs that have kept banks, securities firms and insurance companies from moving into one another's arenas. The proposed deregulation is designed to help American companies expand abroad and become more efficient at home. (*New York Times* 1999)

The legislation is the solution; the Depression-era curbs reference both the problem and its cause; and the help that American companies will receive is the consequence. Notably, this image of a broom sweeping came up five times in the *Times* sample, amounting to once in every three articles. The metaphor emphasised the outdated nature of the old rules.

An alternative narrative

Gramm-Leach-Bliley was approved in the Senate by a vote of 90-8 and it passed the House of Representatives by a vote of 362-57 (Office of the Clerk of the U.S. House of Representatives 1999; United States Senate 1999). Those tallies underscored the political consensus around repealing the old law. The bill was similarly supported by the regulatory community. After its passage, Greenspan said in a speech:

> It is clear that the consumer will benefit from the wider permissible scope of activities by, and the more equal competition among, financial entities. That is why the Federal Reserve actively supported this legislation for so long. (Greenspan 1999)

The legislative effort had been held up by a number of conflicts – such as provisions for minority lending or questions about customer privacy – and these were the focus of some of the reporting. But the main deregulatory substance of the bill was characterised, by almost all of the actors quoted, as a settled matter. In such an environment, it is not surprising that news media offered a narrative that reflected the dominant market liberal paradigm of the day.

This is not to say that an alternative narrative was not available, as the *Times* coverage on the day that Gramm-Leach-Bliley passed makes clear. The *Times* highlighted, in the top third of a lengthy article, that there had been "a handful of dissenters" who drew attention to the question of systemic risk. One of those dissenters turned out to be eerily prescient, at least for those who would later argue that repealing Glass-Steagall had fuelled the crisis:

> "I think we will look back in 10 years' time and say we should not have done this but we did because we forgot the lessons of the past, and that that which is true in the 1930s is true in 2010," said Senator Byron L. Dorgan, Democrat of North Dakota. (Labaton 1999e)

Another Democrat, Senator Paul Wellstone, was quoted saying Congress had "seemed determined to unlearn the lessons from our past mistakes" (Labaton 1999e), calling Glass-Steagall a stabiliser that had insulated commercial banking from other forms of risk.

In this alternative narrative, the problem frame is systemic risk, with financial industry greed acting as the cause and the retention of prudential regulation as the solution. The *Times* article includes this narrative, but it also undercuts it. The piece goes on to quote people treating the risks as overblown and touting the promised benefits of the new law. Furthermore, these two comments represented the only substantial objections to the plan to deregulate in the *Times* sample, apart from issues such as lending to the poor or customer privacy.

Apart from one op-ed article, the *Post* sample also does not seriously consider the systemic risk consequence frame. It references consumer groups that are concerned about the prospect of financial concentration because they see it negative for consumers and question whether savings will be passed on. But the *Post* articles do not entertain the possibility that the original rationale for Glass-Steagall had any remaining merit in terms of preventing systemic risk. The *Post* suggested that because industry had already found ways to work around Glass-Steagall, the new law did not represent a significant change for ordinary people. An article on 23 October 1999 thus characterises the change as partly cosmetic: "For consumers, the disappearance of familiar names in a wave of mergers will be the most immediate effect of the bill" (Day 1999a).

There was one article in the *Washington Post* sample that did seriously consider systemic risk, but it was an opinion piece from a contributor. Robert Kuttner, co-founder and co-editor of *The American Prospect,*[13] noted that Glass-Steagall had been a response to speculative excesses in the 1920s. And, as with Senator Dorgan, his words could be seen as prescient:

> Without government as backstop, our financial system would fall victim to its own speculative impulses. And given that government has to play rescue squad, government also has to set limits on speculation in the first place, lest the taxpayers go broke underwriting bailouts. (Kuttner 1999)

Otherwise, the *Post* sample was silent on the question of risks stemming from striking off a law designed to prevent risks.

The paradigm as prism

The strength of the market liberal paradigm in the late 1990s can be seen in various indicators. One, which was referenced in Chapter 1, was a long-running question that Gallup asked regarding the country's biggest economic threat (Jones 2013).

In 1999, "big business" was seen as the nation's biggest future threat by 24% of those surveyed, while "big government" was seen as the biggest threat by 65%. In other words, respondents appeared far more comfortable with businesses and the market dictating affairs than with the government they had elected. The discrepancy, at the time, was the widest it had ever been. As the 20th century drew to a close, Reagan's

Gallup survey: "In your opinion, which of the following will be the
biggest threat to the country in the future - big business, big labor or
big government?"

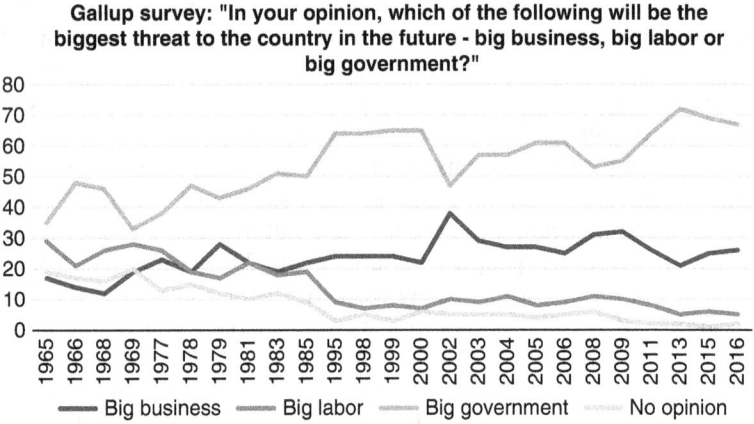

Figure 2.3 Time series of Gallup survey on the nation's top economic threat.

message that government was the problem and not the solution had
become ingrained.

In presenting Glass-Steagall as a problem and deregulation as the
solution, the newspapers advanced narratives that supported the
dominant paradigm of the day. It was not so dominant as to prohibit
consideration of other viewpoints. But those viewpoints were marginalised and dismissed by a parade of other actors who focused on the
benefits that deregulation would bring. Such an environment is in
keeping with the scenario Peter Hall (1993) described for how a
dominant paradigm can act as a prism for policy.

One final point bears considering with regard to Gramm-Leach-
Bliley. While the legislation did attract news coverage, the issue of
financial regulation at the time had little salience, even for those who
might be thought of as having a clear interest in Wall Street developments. Campbell (2010) noted that a Gallup poll in 1999 of
Americans who had at least $10,000 in investable assets showed two-
fifths had heard of the repeal of Glass-Steagall. The journalists who
covered the legislation frequently used dramatic language. They wrote
of how it would "remake" and "overhaul" the country's financial
system; they used terms like "sweeping" and "a new financial era." But
for all that, it seems that even Americans with money to invest did not
pay much attention to financial regulation.

A decade later, they would.

Notes

1 In a review of framing literature, Matthes (2009) found Entman's definition of a frame was most commonly cited. The next most common was from Gamson and Modigliani, who described a frame as "a central organizing idea" (Gamson and Modigliani 1987, p. 143). While Entman focused on the types of frames, Gamson and Modigliani looked at the ways issues were communicated. They saw framing as taking place via "condensing symbols" (1987, p. 143) such as metaphors or catchphrases, which could package a variety of positions into one digestible communication.

2 The cascading activation model was proposed for geopolitical news in the context of 9/11, but I view it as applicable for any complex subject where the public relies on frames from other actors for cues.

3 Entman and Usher (2018) updated the model to factor in social media and digital technology. Actors' use of social media is outside the scope of this analysis, although social media offers potentially fertile ground for future research into narratives and agenda-building.

4 In contrast to Cohen, Kuypers (2009) argues the press has found success at telling people what to think through framing. "Framing involves how the press organizes the context through which the public views its news. At its heart this is a rhetorical process ..." (Kuypers 2009, p. 185).

5 McCombs and others have distinguished between macro- and micro-framing, with macro-framing referring to the main perspective being adopted in a text and micro-framing referring to subsidiary aspects such as linguistic choices, the presence of certain actors or specific content that features in the text.

6 The sample was based on the terms "financial regulation" and "(Dodd or Frank)" and "crisis." The "(Dodd or Frank)" term aimed to capture articles about Dodd-Frank or articles that dealt with financial regulation and quoted one of the lawmakers. It featured 97 articles from the *Washington Post* and 119 from the *New York Times.*

7 Matthes (2009) notes that some studies use the individual proposition as a discourse unit, while others treat entire articles or news items as units. The decision to code on a propositional basis and to use generic frames meant this type of framing methodology was among the rarest of those that feature in the literature.

8 The law left officials with latitude for regulatory rulemaking. During this period, regulatory agencies such as the Commodity Futures Trading Commission and the Securities and Exchange Commission, in consultation with market participants and other stakeholders, began agreeing rules, resulting in a stream of developments that could generate coverage.

9 A tenet of market liberalism is the concept of the self-regulating market, as discussed by Karl Polanyi in *The Great Transformation* (1957). The idea of self-regulation within a market economy is in direct opposition to the interventionist idea that state action is required to steer the market and avoid any harms from unrestrained market competition.

10 The sample was based on a search of articles containing "Glass" and "Steagall."

11 Schiffrin (2011), without going into detail, also observed this tenor in coverage of the repeal of Glass-Steagall, noting a common description of the old law as being outdated.

12 Some have contended the repeal helped cause the crisis of 2008. Bordo (2008) pointed to rapid growth in the non-bank sector after the millennium as a consequence of Glass-Steagall's repeal, noting these institutions held lower capital ratios than traditional commercial banks. "When the crisis hit they were forced to engage in major deleveraging involving the fire sale of assets into a falling market which in turn lowered the value of their assets and those of other financial firms" (Bordo 2008, p. 11). Grant (2010) examined the deregulatory impact that Gramm-Leach-Bliley had on two major banks and made a case for reregulation in the wake of the financial crisis. Crawford (2011) investigated arguments for and against the idea that the repeal helped cause the crisis; she concluded it could not be answered definitively.

13 The magazine has described itself as devoted to promoting "informed discussion on public policy from a progressive perspective" (The American Prospect 2021).

3 Framing the past: The crisis blame game

When the U.S. Congress created an independent commission to investigate the causes of the 2008 financial crisis, it appointed 10 commissioners and hired 87 staff members. They conducted more than 700 interviews, held public hearings and took about 20 months to draw conclusions. Journalists had no such luxury. They were tasked with explaining – instantly and in understandable terms – a highly complex set of events about which there was little consensus.

The commission concluded that there had been widespread failures in regulation and that the crisis was avoidable. Echoing Greenspan's "shocked disbelief" comment (Chapter 1), the commission took aim at one of the tenets of market liberalism. "The sentries were not at their posts, in no small part due to the widely accepted faith in the self-correcting nature of the markets and the ability of financial institutions to effectively police themselves" (Financial Crisis Inquiry Commission 2011, p. xviii).

But as is perhaps inevitable with Congressional inquiries, the findings were heavily politicised. Three of the Republican-appointed commissioners dissented, suggesting that focusing on the amount of regulation was too simplistic. A fourth Republican-appointed commissioner, Peter Wallison of the American Enterprise Institute, offered a separate dissent, arguing that government itself was at fault. Government housing policy, he said, was responsible for creating millions of risky loans, without which the crisis would not have occurred.

The motivation for cause framing often relates directly to solution framing. If an audience can be persuaded about what led to a problem, it stands to reason that they will be more predisposed to solutions that aim to address the root causes given. We can think of cause narratives as solution-priming for an audience. Political actors, independent elites, public advocacy campaigners and the financial industry thus all sought to establish narratives about what led to the upheaval. This

DOI: 10.4324/9781003177944-3

chapter considers how news media wrote about crisis causes and how the framing contributed to broader narratives, based on content analysis and interviews with journalists who covered the crisis. The chapter concludes that while the coverage appeared to support an interventionist narrative, a closer inspection revealed aspects of the framing that weakened the case for paradigm shift.

Three narratives about crisis causes

Many of the actors who opposed a paradigm shift in regulatory policy were worried about expanding government powers, a throwback to Reagan's message. They suggested regulators had proven unable to identify the real causes of the crisis and that many of these factors required less government, not more. This view was rooted in the market liberal idea that concentrating power in the hands of decision-makers (in this case legislators and regulators) was inferior to allowing a market to pick winners and losers. As Martin Baily and Douglas Elliott of Brookings Institution wrote early in the debate, "Regulators are human and prone to errors and if sophisticated market participants fail to see bubbles in the making, how can we expect regulators to see them?" (Baily and Elliott 2009). The critique was not just about a failure to take preventative measures. Some saw errors of judgment as a contributing cause, citing the Federal Reserve's monetary policy in the mid-2000s.

One argument from several think tank authors, led by Wallison, contended that government housing policy prompted the events of 2008. A former White House Counsel who joined AEI just after Gramm-Leach-Bliley was enacted, Wallison had long advocated financial deregulation. Other authors at AEI and the similarly right-leaning Cato Institute published a series of papers within months of Dodd-Frank's passage making this charge (c.f. Kling 2010; Perry and Dell 2010; Rahn 2010). Their arguments centred on the idea that a real estate bubble at the heart of the crisis occurred because of overzealous state efforts to promote homeownership and years of unquestioned political support for two government-sponsored enterprises (GSEs) known as Fannie Mae and Freddie Mac.

Those who made the case for tougher regulation were focused on financial industry behaviour. In the press, "Wall Street bankers" (popular shorthand for all financial industry participants) were portrayed as having a myopic focus on short-term profits and a readiness to game the system bordering on criminality. In policy circles, the discussions were less lurid and more technical, often focusing on issues such as systemic risk and incentives.

These two arguments – the first portraying the state as a cause of the crisis and the second blaming the financial industry – formed the basis for two out of three narratives that Baily and Elliott said initially competed for public acceptance. They listed them as follows:

> Narrative 1: It was the fault of the government, which encouraged a massive housing bubble and mishandled the ensuing crisis.

> Narrative 2: It was Wall Street's fault, stemming from greed, arrogance, stupidity, and misaligned incentives, especially in compensation structures.

> Narrative 3: "Everyone" was at fault: Wall Street, the government, and our wider society. People in all types of institutions and as individuals became blasé about risk-taking and leverage, creating a bubble across a wide range of investments and countries. (Baily and Elliott 2009)

Narrative 1 resisted a paradigm shift, while Narrative 2 advocated 1. Narrative 3 was ambiguous. It supported interventionism in that its spotlight on institutional failures called for a state response. But those who advocated a market liberal paradigm could counter that a society-wide breakdown of responsibility should not lead the state to step in and stifle an otherwise healthy, wealth-creating financial industry.

For Baily and Elliott, Narrative 3 came closest to the truth, although authors at Cato Institute and AEI disputed that.[1] The Brookings authors acknowledge that these narratives required a degree of oversimplification. Still, whatever the downsides of their approach, the framework is helpful in that it shows how developments, trends or situations (as crisis causes) could be treated differently, depending on the narrative on offer. For instance, all actors agreed that government – through action or inaction – had played a part in fomenting the crisis. But some of the same decisions used to argue for Narrative 1 could be repurposed as evidence for Narrative 2. This is what narratives do: they make events fit into a storyline.

The nature of cause framing

Before delving into how elite news media treated the question of what caused the crisis, a more general discussion about cause framing is warranted. The first thing to note is that cause framing was limited. This type of frame was the second least common among frame types that featured in the sample (only frames dealing with moral judgement were rarer). Cause frames represented 9% of the total in the *Washington Post* sample, while moral judgement frames accounted for just below 5%. To put that in perspective, framing in terms of consequences made up 19% of the total, more than twice as common as cause frames. The largest category was solution frames, which accounted for 39%.

The relative paucity of cause frames was to be expected. Tracing the causes of the crisis, or even referring to the causes, created challenges. The subject matter was technical and jargony; there was a lack of consensus on the importance of different factors; and even elite news media have a reputation for rarely going much below the surface when writing about complex issues. All of this suggests problem and solution frames will typically be more common than cause frames. Also, a structural feature of the analysis guaranteed solution frames would dominate the sample; most articles were focused on proposals for, or decisions about, reform (solution frames).

News frames that focused on the causes of the crisis followed the ebb and flow of coverage, but as time went on the news media focused on this issue less. Figure 3.1 shows an initial burst of such framing as the Dodd-Frank bill was unveiled. Cause framing increased as the legislative process gained momentum, leading to the moment Dodd-Frank became law in July 2010. References to the causes of the crisis dwindled from that point on. This shows that actors sought to establish their

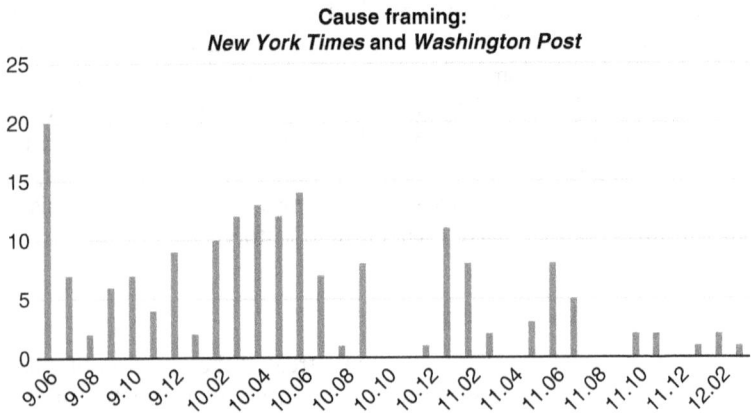

Figure 3.1 Cause framing: *New York Times* and *Washington Post*.

narratives early in the post-crisis period and it indicates the degree to which such framing intensified as the legislative debate unfolded.[2]

Figure 3.1 shows the number of cause frames in the combined *New York Times* and *Washington Post* sample from the introduction of the Dodd-Frank bill to end-March 2012.

Who did most of the framing?

The sample from the *New York Times* and the *Washington Post* featured 180 instances where the cause of the crisis framed discussion. Journalists were the source for the bulk of such framing, accounting for 67%, or two out of every three cause frames. Politicians and government officials were the sources for 21%, and the remaining 12% came from private sector actors, independent elites and advocacy campaigners. Financial industry figures were the sources for only seven cause frames in the sample. The absence of financial industry sources appeared to be by design, as will be discussed later.

Journalists acted as the source of cause frames more than they did for other frame types. This can be partly explained by a particular feature of reporting on causes. It was not uncommon for the cause frames to come in the form of clauses or background sentences that served to give a basic idea as to why a given issue was receiving attention. For instance, in a 22 October 2009 article in the *New York Times*, the journalists wrote:

> On another issue that has been hotly debated for months, the House Agriculture Committee on Wednesday approved a measure to regulate derivatives, the arcane financial instruments that have been linked to the current financial crisis. (Labaton and Stout 2009)

This example draws a connection between derivatives and the crisis, without explaining the linkage. This may come down to the nature of newswriting: reporters and their editors like to avoid slowing down a text or devoting too much space to background detail. But the result is that discussion from journalists of crisis causes was often patchy, vague or undeveloped. In this particular case, the cause frame was coded as unaligned with either paradigm.[3]

Journalists and rhetoric

News journalists are unlike other actor groups in that they typically eschew a rhetorical position and aim for a professional standard of objectivity. This standard, developed over decades (Schudson 2001; Skovsgaard et al. 2013), is in keeping with the notion of a watchdog role. But other actors have different motivations, which show up in their rhetorical approaches. As they compete to shape public narratives, they often aim to appear authoritative. Tactics include providing empirical evidence, developing arguments and deploying rhetorical strategies. News reporters, on the other hand, generally adopt non-emotive language and avoid rhetorical flourishes. If empirical evidence is used, it is generally to provide relevant information, not to develop a rhetorical argument.

This sense of professionalism has implications in terms for how narratives develop. Think tank authors, politicians, campaigners and industry figures may see it as part of their job to promote a narrative, much like a trial lawyer will offer a theory of the case. For reporters, professionalism dictates they avoid doing so. This does not mean some do not seek to create media narratives, and it certainly does not mean journalists do not unintentionally contribute to storylines. Narratives form in the news whether journalists want them to or not.

But if journalists contribute to narratives inconspicuously, how can we systematically identify the contributions? One way is through repetition (Miller and Riechert 2001). The repetition of ideas and perspectives, measured in terms of frames and frame metadata, can point to a narrative's dominance. Given that the sources of many of the frames are other actors, such analysis also can indicate the strength of agenda-building efforts by these actors. While the analysis here is quantitative, one should recognise there are no statistical standards as to what constitutes dominance or significance in terms of frame frequency. But by observing patterns, we can at least determine the relative popularity of one kind of frame versus another.

A skew towards interventionism

The cause framing that did occur skewed heavily toward interventionism. The amount of cause framing in the *Washington Post* and the *New York Times* over identical periods was virtually the same, and the skews towards interventionism were similar in both newspapers. The fact that these two newspapers behaved almost identically suggests that the results of the analysis, specifically the paucity and nature of the frames, could be indicative of wider trends, at least for this news media sub-section.

Table 3.1 Alignment of cause frames

Cause frames	Interventionist	Market liberal	Unaligned	Total
Washington Post	62	8	19	89
New York Times	47	10	34	91
Both newspapers	109	18	52	180

Table 3.1 shows the total numbers of news frames classified as cause frames from the *Washington Post* and *New York Times* samples, with their paradigmatic alignments highlighted.

Interventionist frames outnumbered market liberal frames by more than five to one, meaning that most of the time, journalists or their sources discussed the causes of the financial crisis in terms that were compatible with a paradigm advocating a more pronounced role for the state in regulating finance.

Determining alignment: A close reading

It is useful at this juncture to consider what is meant when we say a cause frame supports an interventionist or market liberal paradigm, or that it is unaligned. Chapter 2 outlined the methodological approach. To explain more about the coding process, I will offer a close reading of the first cause frame that appeared in the sample. It comes from a 6 June 2009 *Washington Post* article headlined "Bank repayments may exceed estimates." In the fourth paragraph, the authors wrote:

> Senior administration officials are considering new rules that would empower regulators to rein in pay practices that are seen as rewarding risky behavior and threatening the stability of banks. (Cho and Appelbaum 2009)

The sentence contains a solution frame (rules that would empower regulators), a problem frame (banking instability) and a cause frame (pay practices that reward risky behaviour). Why is this cause frame aligned with interventionism? In determining alignment, the nature of the cause was the first consideration. If a problem's cause concerned activity that the sentence suggests could or should be governed by the state, without violating some fundamental principle, the frame was likely to be considered aligned with interventionism. In "pay practices," we have an activity linked to a problem (banking instability). The idea of controlling this activity has been mooted in the solution frame (rules to rein in the practice), so the frame at first glance does not suggest a fundamental principle has been violated.

What makes the question of paradigmatic alignment contentious, however, is that there are differing views as to what constitutes a fundamental principle. Many who champion the idea of relying on the collective will of the market rather than state judgment point to Hayek's *The Road to Serfdom* (1944), with his argument that concentrating power in the hands of the state may strip away choices. When the journalists here present the notion – in an unremarkable way – that pay practices could be "reined in," they are framing the discussion in a manner that endorses or at least accepts interventionism. For those who advocate a market liberal paradigm, such an idea is hardly unremarkable: it goes against their view of what the state should be able to do.

A notable feature of this frame is the passive construction of one clause, where the journalists write "are seen as rewarding risky behaviour." The question is: "Seen by whom?" Passive constructions can link a cause and a problem without identifying who has made the linkage. While such constructions can be used for deception (to invent unnamed people who can express an idea on the journalist's behalf, or to imply a view is widely held when that is not necessarily the case), they are often used simply as a shortcut to avoid slowing down the news story with detail. Here, the authors David Cho and Binyamin Appelbaum, or their editors, have decided not to devote extra space to explain the linkage.

Such constructions not only create linkages but also lend them weight through a form of tautology. In absence of detail, the only available answer to the question "Seen by whom?" is: "Seen by those who are critical of Wall Street pay practices." It is a problem for those who see it as a problem. Pro-market advocates may believe dictating pay practices violates a fundamental principle, but their view gets subsumed by the passive construction. These constructions – such as "seen by," "believed to be" or "said to be" – can suggest a consensus or a weight of opinion which may not always be present.

Typically, cause frames involving the private sector were aligned with interventionism. If a cause was related to government, there was a greater chance it would be aligned with market liberalism, as this paradigm highlights the unintended consequences of state measures. Those who subscribe to it see it as their job to make those unintended consequences visible.

Frames can also be classified by what they critique, not just what they themselves assert. For instance, a 3 May 2010 article in the *Times* includes this sentence:

"The activities the administration proposes to restrict did not cause the financial crisis," he said. (Chan 2010)

The speaker is a banking executive. Given the statement's vagueness, one might consider this frame to be unaligned with a paradigm; but the speaker is referring to proposals to restrict proprietary trading and bank size, hence in opposing them he is taking a market liberal stance. Such frames were classified as "wrong target" frames in that they suggest the wrong cause has been identified. A similar case about a state proposal could be seen here:

"This is yet another regulatory cost imposed on the many traditional banks that had nothing to do with causing the financial crisis," said Edward L. Yingling, president of the American Bankers Association. (Yang 2010)

The term "yet another" suggests the state routinely cannot distinguish between real and false causes. The message is aligned with a market liberal paradigm in its critique of the state's limited ability and its implication that the market would not make such a mistake.

Cause breakdown

The paradigmatic alignment of cause framing in aggregate may have been skewed towards interventionism, but analysis of the types of causes that were cited offers a more nuanced reading. The frames ranged from specific causes such as pay, lending standards or rating agency practices, to vague passages about derivatives or references to unspecified causes.

Table 3.2 shows these causes listed in order of frequency in 13 categories. Table 3.3 gives examples of each category, with the paradigmatic alignment of the frame in parentheses in the first column (I for interventionist, ML for market liberal and U for unaligned).

The most common cause was that financial firms engaged in excessive risk-taking; this was in line with Narrative 2 (Wall Street was to blame). But the next three most frequent types were vague and/or highlighted factors such as government behaviour. Together they accounted for more than 40% of all causes given. In other words, elite media focused on both industry and government in writing about crisis causes, including arguments that were made for Narrative 1 such as the role of GSEs and government housing policy. All but one of the 10 references to Fannie Mae and Freddie Mac adopted the government-

Table 3.2 Types of cause frames

Type of cause	Number of references
Excessive risk-taking	41
Unspecified or wide range of causes	37
Lack of oversight/deregulation	23
Derivatives	20
Pay practices	14
Lending practices	12
GSEs and housing policy	10
Rating agency behaviour	8
Wrong target	8
Lack of consumer protection	7
Low capital requirements	5
Regulatory arbitrage	4
Shadow banking	1
Interconnectedness of banks	1

Table 3.3 Cause frame types: Examples

Cause type	Newspaper	Text containing cause frame
Excessive risk-taking (I)	NYT	"These families have seen millions of jobs lost, trillions in savings wiped out, because of the greedy few on Wall Street who gambled with money that didn't even belong to them" (Herszenhorn and Wyatt 2010).
Unspecified causes (U)	WP	The president's speech came on the same day that several large financial firms repaid federal aid, underscoring the administration's transition from fighting a financial crisis to addressing its causes (Appelbaum 2009a).
Lack of oversight (I)	NYT	Mr. Obama told reporters on Tuesday that a "lack of oversight" allowed what he called "wild risk-taking" (Labaton 2009a).
Derivatives (U)	WP	Derivatives trading, which aggravated the financial crisis, has roots in the trading of certain farm commodities, which is why the agriculture committees in the Senate and House have some jurisdiction over it (Dennis and Kane 2010).
Pay practices (I)	WP	There is widespread agreement that many bankers were paid during the boom for

(*Continued*)

Table 3.3 (Continued)

Cause type	Newspaper	Text containing cause frame
		spectacular short-term results achieved by taking massive risks that ultimately produced the global crisis (Appelbaum 2009b).
Lending practices (I)	*NYT*	Its genesis was an article that Ms. Warren wrote a year before the near collapse of the financial system in 2008, a crisis blamed in part on abusive mortgage practices (Calmes and Chan 2010).
GSEs and housing (ML)	*WP*	"Freddie Mac and Fannie Mae were at the heart of the financial crisis," Shelby said Tuesday (Dennis 2010c).
Rating agencies (I)	*NYT*	"We recognize that the misuse of credit ratings, especially in structured finance, contributed importantly to the financial crisis," Mr. Walsh said (Wyatt 2011a).
Wrong target (ML)	*NYT*	"The activities the administration proposes to restrict did not cause the financial crisis," he said (Chan 2010).
Consumer protection (I)	*WP*	Officials have vowed to put in place new rules and regulators to prevent a repeat of the abuses that precipitated the financial crisis (Cho and Dennis 2010a).
Capital requirements (I)	*NYT*	The banks would like us to forget that it was undercapitalized financial institutions that got us into this mess (Norris 2010).
Regulatory arbitrage (I)	*NYT*	Mr. Dodd and others say that the market crisis last year was caused in part by banks that were able to choose which agency would regulate them, and by bank agencies that reduced regulations to encourage more banks to choose them (Labaton 2009b).
Shadow banking (I)	*NYT*	"It is painfully obvious that the financial crisis, which brought us to the brink of international economic collapse, was in large part the result of a 'shadow' or nontransparent financial market," Dennis M. Kelleher, the chief executive of Better Markets, wrote in a comment letter (Morgenson 2011).
Banking connections (U)	*NYT*	The crisis was made worse by the interdependence of many of the largest financial outfits (Wyatt 2011b).

caused-the-crisis line, with the one exception highlighting how the GSEs prevented more damage from being done. Another way to look at the data: Frames that focused on financial industry behaviour represented less than half of the total number of cause frames.

The coverage, in emphasising the government and structural factors along with the financial industry, suggest an embrace of Narrative 3. Given the strength of public animosity towards the financial sector in 2009, it is understandable that the Brookings authors, and many others, believed news media were advancing Narrative 2.[4] But a close examination of the coverage over an extended period indicates otherwise, at least for these elite news media providers.

The view from the newsroom

To consider the results of the content analysis, I interviewed 14 journalists who had covered the crisis and its aftermath for elite news organisations.[5] These included national newspapers, international news organisations and newspaper chains. Most covered the regulatory story as their beat, although the interviews included general news reporters who only occasionally covered regulation. This allowed comparisons between specialist and non-specialist journalistic responses to some of the issues that arose.

The interviewees covered the crisis for Bloomberg, the *Financial Times*, Gannett, McClatchy, the *New York Times*, Reuters and the *Wall Street Journal*. Some went on to work for other elite news groups, including Dow-Jones, Politico, *USA Today* and the *Washington Post*. The interviewees represented a cross-section of journalists recognised by their peers as having the highest standards in the field; among them were two Pulitzer Prize winners and two other Pulitzer Prize finalists. For this chapter, the interviews focused on three themes: Narratives about what caused the crisis, challenges from writing about the causes and editorial choices concerning sources. I began by asking what they thought were the dominant narratives in the coverage. Many of their responses pointed to Narrative 3.

David Enrich, now at the *New York Times*, covered the U.S. regulatory story for the *Wall Street Journal* between 2008 and 2010. He dismissed the idea that home ownership policy led to the crisis (Narrative 1), adding that this was factually wrong and that it deliberately ignored much of the problem. Instead, he said "a zillion things" caused the crisis and he offered a slightly scatological account that clung closely to Narrative 3.

I can go through those zillion things ... It was ranging from homeowners that were being greedy and stupid and reckless and taking on much more debt than they could afford, to slightly up the food chain, then mortgage brokers who were encouraging them to do this and to the originators who were providing these reckless loans and then up the food chain to the Wall Street firms that were buying these mortgages and the rating agencies that were rating the shit that they cobbled together, to the stupid investors all over the world who were buying the shit, to the regulators who were turning a blind eye to this massive risk (inaudible) all over the financial system to the politicians who were clamouring for more Americans to have homes to the politicians who were pushing for completely laissez-faire regulation to the media.

Kevin Hall, who was the national economics correspondent for McClatchy from 2005 to 2013, was a Pulitzer finalist for his reporting on the causes of the crisis (he later won the prize for coverage of organised crime and corruption). He had covered financial crises in other countries as well. He broadly subscribed to the narrative that everybody was at fault but said that was weighted more towards banks.

If you go back and look at why we got to where we did, every step along the way something was broken, whether it was the underwriting, whether it was the non-bank lending, whether it was the regulators unaware of the interconnectedness of this growth and these non-bank lenders, nobody really understanding structured finance, because that was pretty new.

Part of his reason for weighting the banks' culpability more heavily was because he felt they should have known better. Hall cited an often-quoted line from Charles Prince, who ran Citigroup in 2007, when he spoke about the need to keep dancing as long as the music was playing.[6] "I think nobody wanted to be the first to back out of something where they were making a lot of money, and they all knew was going to end badly," Hall said.

The interviews included two general assignment reporters for Gannett, based in Washington during the Dodd-Frank debate. Ledyard King, one of them, said there may have been excessive lending and shoddy practices, but he also suggested borrowers shared some of the blame.

I'm personally, I think, a fairly conservative financial person. I don't borrow more than I think I can pay. And leading up to the crash were people who were – I mean they were obviously duped into thinking they could borrow more, but I also think the consumers you know, it was what the consumers wanted to hear. They wanted to buy the house ... the five-bedroom house in a nice neighbourhood, they wanted to own a Mercedes.

Stephen Labaton, twice a Pulitzer finalist, covered regulation for the *New York Times*. He had a personal thesis as to the crisis cause, one that focused heavily on the government's actions.

I came to Washington in 1990 to cover the savings and loan crisis for the *New York Times*, which was about a $120 billion bailout, and we all thought that would be the biggest crisis we'd ever see in our lifetimes. If you study financial crises throughout American history, you will notice that often the seeds of every major crisis are sown in a previous crisis. Regulations and laws are adopted that seek to address the particular issues of a crisis and often they create a new set of circumstances that contribute to the next crisis.

This theory suggests a degree of government culpability that goes well beyond what was portrayed in the Congressional report, which had focused on problems stemming from deregulation rather than from any active steps that government took.

The challenge of writing about causes

Elite news media tend to be staffed with experienced, knowledgeable reporters. They appeared to be within their comfort zone when writing about what led to the crisis. Some expressed confidence based on their experience and the degree to which their organisations encouraged them to dig deeply into underlying issues. What they didn't know, they worked hard to learn about. But they said the crisis still presented challenges.

Caren Bohan, who covered the White House for Reuters during the Dodd-Frank debate and later became the Washington editor at *USA Today*, recalled:

I guess I felt pretty confident in my knowledge of the general causes of it, because I'd been an economics reporter for so long. I remember seeing the excesses building, and I had covered the economy during a recession before ... . I also tried to read a lot about it, about what was happening behind the scenes, at Lehman and at Bear Stearns, I tried to understand, as much as I could, the series of events that played out.

Labaton said the *New York Times* encouraged him to be a student of history and he felt he brought perspective as someone with experience covering what he called "the intersection of Wall Street and Washington." Still, he said the ferocity of the crisis underlined the importance and difficulty of understanding it fully. "No one in our lifetimes, in my lifetime, had ever experienced a financial crisis of that magnitude with those implications."

Many of the journalists did not have the benefit of historical perspective. Francesco Guerrera, who covered Dodd-Frank for the *Financial Times* at the time, said one structural difficulty is that journalists are very good at looking at the present and at the recent past, but many are too young to know enough about events further back.

We were all like looking back and trying to educate ourselves as fast as we could or ask people who were there. But then again, if you ask people, they had a point of view or a biased point of view. So that was the most difficult part, when they were saying, 'It was all because of, you know, the repeal of Glass-Steagall,' or the regulation of this, or even go back to even before, the fixed rate mortgage market in the U.S.

Tight deadlines and the speed of events added to the pressure. Guerrera, like Labaton, said the magnitude of the crisis affected journalists. He said that as much as they may wallow in self-importance and talk about writing "the first draft of history," most of the time they are not doing that. The 2008 crisis was an exception.

What I know of the people who covered the crisis, and lived through the crisis, that is a very reflective bunch. We were faced, for the first time in our career, and maybe for the last time in our career, with a very huge responsibility. There's a huge responsibility when you're writing, as I had to do, the splash in the *Financial Times*, the night that Lehman fell.

Asked about how they coped with often radically different accounts for what was at the heart of the crisis, several journalists said they spoke to as many sources as possible and then simply made the call.

"General journalistic rules apply. So, you listen to them all, and then you try to present them all, or making a judgment as to which are the good ones or the bad ones," Guerrera said.

Tom Braithwaite covered post-crisis regulatory issues from Washington for the *Financial Times*. He made a similar comment: "I think, you speak to as many people as possible, and you interrogate who seems credible or otherwise." Braithwaite said this approach required considering the sources' agendas: "Whenever you're speaking to anyone, as a journalist you're hopefully treating them sceptically and working out what the perspective lies beneath what they're doing."

Another issue was how to make the writing accessible. David Herszenhorn, who covered Dodd-Frank for the *New York Times* and now writes for Politico, said:

> The challenge that's posed by a subject like financial regulation is that it's so complex, I mean, and for the average reader it's almost meaningless in a way ... They know that there was a financial crisis, they know that their houses, their mortgages, ended up under water in some way. But getting at the root causes of it, you know, was really, really hard.

Hall of McClatchy related an incident when he saw coverage in the *Wall Street Journal* about GSEs which he felt needed follow-up. He pitched an idea to his editor but was rebuffed. Hall recalled: "And he (the editor) said, 'No, this is too complex, people's eyes are going to glaze over.'" In this case, Hall went around his direct editor and spoke to the investigative editor.

> We did a lot of reporting initially on the crisis and then the question was, what do you do beyond the daily stuff and the Hill stuff ... . This isn't a criticism of my editor. My editor was just one of the guys who was more focused on daily coverage and how we cover the next turn on this. And I, having covered these things in other countries, thought the greater value was telling a bigger picture.

What emerges from these accounts is a journalistic corps that felt confident in their ability to dissect what had happened, but were at times daunted by such a complicated, impactful story. Making immediate sense of the crisis posed challenges, from gaining the requisite knowledge quickly to speaking to a wide-enough array of sources to writing the story in terms that would be widely understood. This picture helps explain the limited amount of cause framing and the vague or basic nature of many cause references. It supports the analysis about how news media differed from other actors in discussing crisis causes. Ultimately, the weight of the story and the resulting need to focus on immediate problems, coupled with the difficulties of explaining the crisis's origins to a wide audience, appeared to dissuade reporters from spending too much time and energy trying to rake over the past.

Conspicuous by their absence

Financial industry figures and independent elites were the sources for just 4% each of the already limited number of cause frames in the sample. The modest number of independent elites is all the more striking given the expertise they offer and the complexity of the story at hand. In the case of financial industry figures, they were keen to avoid the media spotlight at this time, but it is noteworthy nonetheless given that much of the subject matter in regulatory news articles concerned these sources themselves.

In Chapter 1, Robert Litan of Brookings spoke of how journalists had stopped calling experts after the crisis. But with figures from the financial industry, it would appear that their absence in the media represented a strategic objective on their part to not appear in news media rather than a collective choice made by journalists. Journalists who covered the story, however, said the industry was still active in trying to steer discourse behind the scenes, both with media and other actors. I spoke with a financial industry communications strategist who explained the logic. The best communications strategy, he suggested, involved avoiding media and concentrating on interacting directly with political actors.

Enrich of the *New York Times* also noticed this effort to stay out of the news. "All these groups, and the banks individually, and the bank executives individually, were trying to keep a much lower public profile. They did not want their names attached to things," he said. But it would be a mistake, he added, to assume that just because their names were not in stories, that they were not engaging with media. He said "there was, and remains, like, an army of these people" who would talk on a not-for-attribution basis every day.

Politico's Herszenhorn said financial industry efforts were focused mostly on lawmakers, where the industry felt it might have a more sympathetic audience.

> They (legislators) are really susceptible, right? 'Here's a campaign donation and hey, we would really like this, which we say is going to do X, Y or Z' … If the competing interest isn't there, pushing

back, who will, right? It's a much more dangerous issue when it comes to influencing the policymakers, but of course you know, look, they try very hard to influence also the pundits, right, the people who are going to take a position.

Herszenhorn said industry representatives were aware that pushing a message with a Congressional reporter for the *New York Times* was likely to be met with scepticism. Enrich, however, said that while industry figures knew that hard-sell tactics were unlikely to work, that did not mean they did not try to shape the way journalists saw the story. A problem he noted – which was highlighted in post-crisis literature – was the level of expertise that journalists had, which limited their ability to push back on assertions.

> Some journalists, as they get more experience, become experts in a subject matter they're covering in a really nuanced, technical way. But for the most part we're not … . The institutions have people who are most sophisticated about this, who are being paid a lot of money to kind of get their ideas and their viewpoints and perspectives into the brains of journalists. And not in a way where it's like a sledgehammer, right? They're trying to just kind of shape the way you view the world.

Guerrera said that the industry's behind-the-scenes work enabled it to persuade some politicians to push for less-stringent regulation.

> The immediate effect of the crisis disappeared from the public's mind, and then something as complex as Dodd-Frank started being discussed in Congress and committees. And the issues discussed in Dodd-Frank are really not household issues. It's very difficult to explain the Volcker Rule to someone who doesn't know the financial sector. So, all of the sudden there was a license, for the people who wanted … to soften up the legislation.

Herszenhorn also noted that lobbying could lead to legislative provisions that were not always obvious. What worried him most about legislative efforts, he said, were the issues that did not come across his radar. If it was a well-discussed issue, there was less concern, even if the issue was highly technical: "If it's on my radar I'm going to find people to teach me – that's what I do for a living."

The communications strategist I interviewed said that when financial institutions did speak publicly, either individually or via industry associations, they mostly stuck to a script that read: We didn't see it coming. His clients included financial institutions and he asked that his comments be treated anonymously. He said banks knew they could not be vocal about post-crisis regulation because they had just taken tens of billions of dollars of taxpayers' money.

> The general line that most financial services companies took was, nobody saw this coming. … Everybody from the government, to Congress, to mortgage originators, to mortgage securitisation shops, and everybody involved, had something to answer for. But what they all had in common and what they all felt they could say appropriately was, nobody could forecast the severity of the crisis that hit. That I think was the common refrain.

An example of that occurred in testimony by a prominent banking industry leader. Officials for the Financial Services Roundtable were called to testify before Senate and Congressional committees at least 13 times between June 2009 and March 2012, the timeframe for this study. Transcripts showed the subject of what caused the crisis was brought up by a group official just once. On 15 July 2009, Financial Services Roundtable Chief Executive Officer Steven Bartlett told the House Financial Services Committee:

> The focus of this hearing is on the future, as it should be, but I'm going to begin with an apology about the past. I've said this at other times and other forums and in other places for perhaps over a year. John Dalton, representing the Roundtable and Housing Policy Council, said this the last time he was before the committee, and that is our sincere – my personal, sincere apologies – (inaudible) – our organisations for the role that we played and I played in failing to see the crisis in time to help avert it. So I accept my responsibilities. (U.S. House Committee on Financial Services 2009b)

Bartlett added there was "a lot of blame to go around, a lot of sources of the problem." He argued the biggest problem was "a regulatory system that is in chaos in terms of its structure." The testimony, despite the carefully worded "apology," was consistent with Narrative 1. He stopped short of accepting that financial companies bore responsible for causing the crisis, only for not *seeing it in advance* so that they could warn others. He suggests the government's regulatory system was a bigger problem.

A rearguard action

Four conclusions were drawn from the research. Firstly, in writing about the causes of the crisis, elite media framed discussion mostly in line with an interventionist paradigm. The post-crisis coverage was markedly different, in tone and substance, from news coverage from a decade earlier. But there are caveats. Cause framing featured in the sample less than most other types of framing; and when such frames did appear, many were vague.

Secondly, news framing was less anti-Wall Street than many observers suggested. Think tank authors from Brookings to Cato to AEI had the impression that news media primarily blamed the financial industry for the 2008 crisis. When I reached out to Wallison, for example, he was critical of U.S. news media for suggesting the issue boiled down to not enough oversight of the industry. In an email interview, he said news media "adopted the simple story that it was the result of insufficient regulation of the financial system" and that any other explanation was not given credence. Wallison believed his views about the cause of the crisis did not take hold with media for two reasons: "First, because it seems obvious to the media mind that every problem can be solved by more regulation, and second, because trying to understand another explanation takes too much work."

While the coverage placed much of the blame with the industry, the data overall were not supportive of Narrative 2. Government behaviour and vague systemic factors were regularly cited as causes. Furthermore, financial industry behaviour was listed as a crisis cause in less than half the total number of frames, while the housing policy narrative that was aggressively pushed by right-leaning think tanks did get some modest media attention.

Thirdly, discourse from news media lined up with more centrist actors and eschewed radical positions. Polemic discourse offered by advocacy campaigners, or by some in the think tank community, found purchase. But overall, the sample showed an aversion to lining up squarely behind any single theory of crisis causation. Notably, the sample reflected more wariness of the principles of interventionism than the state actors who authored or supported the conclusions of the Financial Crisis Inquiry Commission report.

Repeated allusions in the interviews to journalistic standards, in terms of research and source-gathering, account for a readiness and desire to include a wide range of views and to avoid aligning with any single line of thinking in terms of crisis causes. The complexity of the situation, even for reporters who had been on this beat for some time, warranted a cautious approach that called for speaking to as many sources as possible.

Fourthly, agenda-building efforts were visible not only based on what appeared in the coverage, but also what was omitted. Financial industry figures were conspicuous in their absence as sources, by-passing news media and targeting more direct forms of agenda-building. The financial community understood that the environment was not conducive to vocal PR efforts. When compelled to speak publicly, such as in Congressional hearings, industry figures relied on the nobody-saw-it-coming line.

This fourth conclusion is most intriguing from an agenda-building perspective. Journalists were well aware of efforts by financial industry figures to avoid the glare of the media spotlight while still pushing their agenda behind the scenes. Meanwhile, the nobody-saw-it-coming line these actors used served a dual purpose. It deflected blame, while serving to undermine the state and any suggestion that government was equipped to identify the important issues.

Judging from the number of times that news reports featured the "excessive risk" cause frame, it appears that journalists were not persuaded by the nobody-saw-it-coming line. What is more, the comments in the interviews suggested few in the news media were prepared to give financial industry figures much benefit of the doubt. Still, this idea found a faint echo in the inclusion of "wrong target" cause frames, which also suggested the state lacked the capacity to identify what really mattered. The comments also prompt a question as to how much attention was devoted – or should have been devoted – to investigating these behind-the-scenes efforts to influence state actors.

The desire for interventionism from many actors in the early days after the crisis was strong. But that did not translate into a clear media narrative that called for focusing on reining in the financial industry. The emphasis on vague, systemic factors in the coverage and the comments offered in interviews suggests that news media were prepared to entertain a wide variety of factors beyond those that targeted Wall Street. Efforts to forge a public discourse that favoured paradigm shift had begun. But those promoting a market liberal paradigm had mounted a rearguard action.

Notes

1 Brookings authors were often interventionist in their crisis-related positions while being sympathetic to market liberal arguments, as Baily and Elliott were in their paper. This is in line with the think tank's reputation as a

centrist institution and is supported by findings from Groseclose and Milyo (2005) based on a method that ranks think tanks and other policy groups ideologically according to a system known as ADA scoring. Developed by Americans for Democratic Action to determine the relative ideological position of legislators, this method is a common measure of political ideology (Bishin 2003).

2 The data reflect the amount of coverage Dodd-Frank received at key junctures. After taking that into account, the focus on establishing the cause of the crisis was highest early on, with most news stories in the initial months of coverage containing a higher-than-average number of references to the cause of the crisis, and most stories in later months containing a lower-than-average number of such references.

3 The use of the term "arcane" could be read negatively and suggestive of a need for greater oversight. The passage, however, was ambiguous. A conservative approach was taken to coding; unambiguous text was needed to indicate alignment.

4 Subsequent quantitative analysis by Schranz and Eisenegger (2011) looked at front-page articles by the *New York Times*, the *Guardian* and Swiss daily *Neue Zürcher Zeitung* from 2007 to 2009 and found that banks and their chief executives accounted for between 70% and 80% of the references to crisis culprits. The share of references to government as a crisis cause initially was negligible, although it rose to just below 10% by the second half of 2009.

5 I also interviewed think tank authors from AEI and Brookings, as well other actors who sought to shape post-crisis discourse, such as Heather Booth, former director of AFR.

6 "When the music stops, in terms of liquidity, things will be complicated. But as long as the music is playing, you've got to get up and dance. We're still dancing," Prince told the *Financial Times* (Nakamoto and Wighton 2007).

4 Framing the future: The consequences of regulation

A theme in early post-crisis discourse was the idea that the government had to perform a balancing act. The thinking went like this: On one hand, financial markets had just imploded and caused chaos, so the scope for systemic risk needed to be addressed; on the other hand, the economy was on its knees, so efforts to tackle systemic risk needed to avoid damaging the economy further. Within that discussion, the concept of banks being "too big to fail" (TBTF) became a talking point. Systemic risk is a nebulous concept for many people, but TBTF felt intuitive. People could grasp the moral and economic ramifications of a bank being able to hold the government hostage. The scope for TBTF institutions to come into existence, and the question of what to do when this happened, were considered by many regulators to be among the most important – and by some to be *the* most important – of issues requiring attention. The TBTF issue also was intrinsically connected with a major flashpoint in public discourse, the taxpayer-funded bailouts of large financial firms. Virtually everyone seemed to agree that having to bail out banks for their bad decisions was not desirable; but there were sharp disagreements about whether the state should intervene with stricter regulation to prevent future bailouts, or whether market forces should act as a disciplinary mechanism.

This chapter considers this balancing act theme by focusing on consequence framing. Consequence framing here refers to efforts – by journalists or other actors quoted – to frame discussion in terms of future policy impacts. Such framing may be part of a wider narrative strategy, such as efforts to list or quantify costs and benefits, or to identify winners and losers from a policy proposal (c.f. McBeth et al. 2007). Political actors in particular have strong incentives for framing issues in terms of the future. So long as experts are divided over the likely impacts of a policy, it becomes nearly impossible to dismiss someone's predictions. There is a weak feedback mechanism at play since it typically takes a long time for

DOI: 10.4324/9781003177944-4

people to experience the effects of a policy decision, by which time the original claims have been long forgotten. Political actors thus may feel emboldened to make predictions, with little worry that those claims will be remembered or linked to later outcomes. Jennifer Jerit, a political scientist, calls these "predictive appeals" (Jerit 2009, p. 412) and says they have been an understudied phenomenon within framing literature, despite their abundance in political communication. I will examine such predictive appeals by looking at the framing of the consequences of regulation. This aspect of political communication formed a linchpin of agenda-building efforts to thwart a regulatory paradigm shift.

The research finds that a range of actors worked in concert to promote a market liberal paradigm with increasing strength and sophistication soon after the crisis. These efforts proved successful as market liberal framing dominated the news sample. What is more, awareness of actors' agenda-building efforts did not necessarily provide a defence against those efforts. Journalists with extensive experience and deep specialist knowledge had a clear sense of when sources were trying to use spin. And yet, a pattern still emerged that favoured a paradigm that had just been brought into question by the crisis.

The chapter begins with an overview of the concept of TBTF, a deceptively complex term. I offer a policy framework for thinking about TBTF and describe two narratives that emerged. I next discuss the results of the content analysis, concerning both TBTF and the broader issue of the consequences of regulation. Finally, we will hear from journalists who covered the story to consider what may have accounted for the results of the content analysis.

Bank size: An issue too big to ignore

Sheila Bair, chair of the Federal Deposit Insurance Corp from June 2006 to July 2011, cited TBTF as the most pressing issue requiring attention. "It is at the top of the list of things that need to be fixed," she was quoted as saying in a 2009 article in the *Washington Post* (Cho 2009). To judge whether Bair's assessment was shared in the think tank community, and to see what other issues attracted attention there, I reviewed think tank literature over an extended period. Table 4.1 shows rankings from the *Global Go To Think Tank Index Report* (McGann 2009, 2010, 2011, 2012) for economic policy think tanks for four years following the crisis.

The last column shows the five lowest cumulative totals among institutions in the report, making them the five highest-ranked institutions over the total four-year period.

Table 4.1 Think tank rankings

Institution	2009	2010	2011	2012	Total
Brookings Institution	1	1	1	1	4
Cato Institute	2	3	3	2	10
National Bureau of Economic Research	5	2	2	4	13
Peterson Institute for International Economics	4	5	4	5	18
American Enterprise Institute	3	4	10	3	20

A Google search of these institutions' website domains, using the terms "regulation," "Dodd" and "Frank," identified 73 publications between 1 June 2009 and 31 December 2012.[1] The following issues (in alphabetical order) regularly came up:

1   **Consumer protection:** This concerns the role of consumers in the crisis and a view among some that protection was needed from predatory firms.
2   **Government housing market activity:** This concerns the role of government sponsorship of home loan agencies in influencing lenders and borrowers.
3   **Investor protection:** A perceived lack of investor protection in the event of a TBTF event featured in post-crisis debate due to the scope for systemic risk.
4   **Regulation of non-bank firms:** This relates to TBTF. The near collapse of American Insurance Group and other non-bank firms during the crisis made this a point of discussion.
5   **Systemic incentives:** This is an umbrella term for incentives for market participants to take on historically high levels of risk. Examples ranged from banks' bonus culture and short-termism to credit rating agency business models.
6   **TBTF institutions and capital requirements:** This refers to the notion that the failure of certain firms could endanger the financial system and the view that regulators should focus on the capital adequacy of the banking industry. It included discussion about public funds potentially being needed for private sector firms that threatened the financial system.
7   **Transparency:** This concerns the dearth of information regarding swathes of financial activity. Observers noted that neither the state nor the marketplace had centralised sources of information concerning derivatives contracts worth hundreds of billions of

dollars, meaning regulators and market participants had been flying blind before the crisis.

These discussion points closely tracked the legislative debate itself. All of the above issues, with the exception of government housing market activity, ultimately were addressed in one way or another in the Dodd-Frank law. Table 4.2 shows how often they featured as a focus in those publications, based on my review.

The leading economic think tanks, like Bair and the drafters of the Dodd-Frank bill, saw TBTF and systemic incentives as among the most pressing of issues. But the think tanks had very different ideas about policy. As I will discuss later, they lined up behind two narratives. One called for the state to adopt policies that identified and addressed TBTF-related risks. The other called for dismissing the concept of TBTF altogether and letting the market decide whether banks that were teetering should survive.

History of TBTF as a concept

The phrase "too big to fail" became closely associated with the 2008 crisis after the U.S. government, facing significant market distress following Lehman's collapse, injected cash into several large financial institutions. A worldwide search on Google Trends showed searches for the acronym spiking in the spring of 2008, as the government engineered a bailout of investment bank Bear Stearns, an event that presaged the wider upheaval.

But TBTF as a concept had been in existence for nearly a quarter-century by that point, and its origins go back even further, to a policy shift in 1950 by the Federal Depository Insurance Corp (Dymski 2011;

Table 4.2 Issue frequency in think tank sample

Issue	Number of publications that highlighted the issue
Systemic incentives	33
Too big to fail/capital requirements	31
Government housing market activity	25
Transparency	11
Consumer protection	10
Investor protection	5
Regulation of non-bank firms	4

Morgan and Stiroh 2005). Before then, U.S. regulators' options in the event of an imminent bank failure were to shutter the firm and pay off deposits that were insured, or to facilitate an acquisition by another bank that would assume the stricken bank's liabilities. In 1950, the government decided it could support a bank if its continued operation was deemed "essential" (Dymski 2011, p. 5). That third option was what occurred in the early 1980s when the government injected capital into Continental Illinois Bank, then the nation's seventh-largest bank. The bank had pursued an aggressive growth strategy that left it with large bad debts.

As a matter of historical record, there is disagreement as to who coined the term "too big to fail," although not when it first occurred.[2] One figure from a 1984 Congressional hearing who used it, and who has been cited in some cases as its originator, was Congressman Stewart B. McKinney:

> Mr. Chairman, let us not bandy words. We have a new kind of bank. It is called too big to fail. TBTF, and it is a wonderful bank. (U.S. House Committee on Banking, Finance and Urban Affairs 1984, p. 300)

McKinney's use of the acronym is striking as it seems to anticipate a time when the concept would become well known. TBTF generated political and regulatory discussion in the mid-1980s, and academic analysis over the ensuing two decades. But it was not until the events surrounding the 2008 crisis that the term gained widespread public currency.[3]

Despite its apparent simplicity, TBTF is a complex concept. It can refer to (1) a policy to prevent the failure of an institution, or (2) a status conferred on a firm, where it is believed that the state would not allow it to fail (Dymski 2011). Furthermore, questions about policy can be about either preventing or reacting to the collapse of an institution. Whether referring to policy or status, TBTF is associated with a range of problems. Four of the largest are as follows:

> **Systemic risk:** This is the risk of catastrophic disruption from the hypothetical failure of institutions due to their interconnectedness with other firms and the possibility of contagion.
> **Moral hazard:** This is when a widespread belief that the government will step in to prevent a failure leads to bad behaviour (e.g., excessive risk-taking).

Marketplace distortions: This refers to the effects from market participants believing a TBTF policy is in place or will be adopted. Firms which have been deemed to have the status of TBTF can obtain lower borrowing costs than their rivals, based on the presumption that the government will cover their debts if need be. **Unfairness to taxpayers:** This stems from the cost of government bailouts in the event of an institution's collapse. Two factors fuel the perceived unfairness. One is due to the financial burden potentially being placed on people who were unconnected to the causes of the collapse. Another is the wealth disparity between average citizens and highly paid executives at banks receiving bailouts.[4]

All four problems come up regularly in political economy literature about TBTF and they are interrelated. Moral hazard can result in a distorted marketplace, which can increase systemic risk by encouraging more risk-taking. That in turn can increase the likelihood of taxpayer-funded support in the event of trouble.

TBTF could be used with reference to any one of the problems above. When President Obama announced support for the so-called Volcker Plan, in January 2010 as part of the Dodd-Frank legislation, he said: "Never again will the American taxpayer be held hostage by a bank that is 'too big to fail'" (White House Office of the Press Secretary 2010). Obama's hostage metaphor focuses attention on three actors – the bank, the taxpayer and the government – and invokes both the bank's TBTF *status* and the government's intention of avoiding a TBTF *policy*. The comment speaks to the problem of unfairness to taxpayers, although his full remarks referenced the other three TBTF problems.

Given so many different ways to consider TBTF, discussions about policy can become muddled. The following framework for discussing the intersection of TBTF *policy* and TBTF *status* considers options before a bank has reached TBTF status (A1–A4) and once such a status has been reached (B1–B4).

Main policy options *before* a bank achieves TBTF status
A1 Minimal state regulation, with minimal focus on bank size or systemic importance
A2 Minimal state regulation and a ban on corporate bailouts
A3 Measures to prevent firms from becoming TBTF, without ruling out bailouts
A4 Measures to prevent firms and a ban on corporate bailouts

Main policy options *after* a bank achieves TBTF status and is deemed to be at risk

B1 No state action, leaving the market to decide the bank's fate

B2 State-run administration, leading to liquidation, break-up or nationalisation

B3 State-sponsored rescue with punitive terms

B4 State-sponsored rescue without punitive terms

The post-2008 debate involved combinations of the eight policy positions (and possibly others), based on events and counterfactual analysis. The positions line up with different paradigms. A market liberal paradigm calls for A1, A2 and B1, while an interventionist paradigm suggests A3, B2, B3 and B4. A4 is a hybrid option in that it calls for interventionism before a bank achieves TBTF status, but a market liberal policy if a bank somehow does still reach that status.

The broadness of the TBTF concept means it can represent radically different ideas for different actors. Actors as far apart ideologically as AEI and the public advocacy group Americans for Financial Reform have referenced TBTF in highly critical terms, with each referring to different policies and holding different views about the efficacy of one paradigm versus another (c.f. Americans for Financial Reform 2009; Wallison 2012). Such distinctions between status and policy or between any of the eight positions are typically missing in news media accounts.

Applying the TBTF framework

Before the collapse of Lehman, the state broadly followed the A1 option (minimal regulation). It then became erratic when faced with firms that had achieved TBTF status. The state intervened to subsidise a takeover deal for Bear Stearns months before Lehman (Baker and McArthur 2009) in an example of B4 (rescue without punitive terms). It then sought to take a tougher stance with a B1 policy (no state support) for Lehman, before switching back to B4 for other banks and insurer AIG once the fallout from the Lehman decision became apparent.

Based on the Overton Window notion that links policy legitimacy to public opinion,[5] the Bush administration had reason to believe it might have erred in rescuing Bear Stearns. A Gallup Poll in March 2008 showed that 61% of Americans opposed the federal government taking steps to prevent Wall Street investment firms from failing (Jacobe 2008). This came after a Senate committee hearing, in which administration officials were sharply questioned about the TBTF concept and in which U.S. Federal Reserve Chairman Ben Bernanke defended the rescue (United States Senate Committee on Banking, Housing and Urban Affairs 2008).

Dodd-Frank adopted a version of A3 (measures to prevent banks from reaching TBTF status). It adopted one significant B2-related measure called the Orderly Resolution Authority, while leaving open the possibility of B3 or B4 policies if TBTF concerns dictated. Dodd-Frank did not ban bailouts (A4), although protracted debate led to language that set limits on how public funds could be used for supporting private sector firms. Michael Barr of Brookings saw the Orderly Resolution Authority as a significant innovation: "Before Dodd-Frank, the government did not have the authority to unwind large, highly leveraged, and substantially interconnected financial firms that failed – such as Bear Stearns, Lehman Brothers, and AIG – without disrupting the broader financial system" (Barr 2011).

But the government rejected a more draconian version of the interventionist B2 policy option when carrying out its rescue programme. Historian Adam Tooze, reviewing the crisis on its 10-year anniversary, saw this as evidence of a reluctance to embrace a more decisive policy shift. "The kind of deep conservativism of the crisis response can be measured by the fact that none of the big banks were broken up," he told an interviewer (Slate 2018). Unlike policymakers in Europe, U.S. politicians and regulators seemed to dismiss the possibility of bank nationalisation, even on a temporary basis. In Britain, for instance, Northern Rock and Bradford & Bingley were fully nationalised, while the government took a majority stake in Royal Bank of Scotland and stakes in other firms as a result of the crisis (Parliament. House of Commons 2009).

Consequential narratives

Chapter 3 used the narratives identified by Brookings to explore discussion about the causes of the crisis. In this chapter, I will adopt the same approach, offering my own narrative summaries about TBTF, based on the language used in think tank reports, political speeches and news articles. Narrative 1 makes the case for a market liberal paradigm and Narrative 2 for an interventionist one.

Narrative 1: Let the market do its job
Measures to constrain banks, such as higher capital requirements, may not be effective and will harm businesses and taxpayers. The belief among banks that the state would always rescue them had

induced many to act recklessly, so interventionism will only cause more bailouts. An outright ban on bailouts is needed to convince firms to act responsibly. No bank should be considered too big to fail, and whatever pain is felt from a collapse will serve to reinforce market principles.

Narrative 2: The system is broken
Banks have shown they cannot oversee themselves. Without state intervention, banks will inevitably become TBTF again, eventually jeopardising the economy and requiring more bailouts. That would be a far higher cost than any economy-dampening effect from tighter regulation. Higher capital adequacy levels and other preventive measures are needed. The crisis also has shown that not offering support for systemically important firms when they are in trouble is a recipe for disaster.

Both narratives are forward-looking (in line with consequence framing) and focused on policy efficacy. Democrats embraced Narrative 2, as seen in Obama's previously cited comment about the Volcker Plan. Early in the legislative process, House Financial Services Committee Chairman Barney Frank called for preventive measures, in line with the A3 option described earlier:

> It (TBTF) should not exist, and if we do this job right, it will not exist. Part of our major core set of principles here is – and legislation – first, to set up a set of regulations that will keep people from getting too big to fail, in part by severe limitations on leverage. There will be at several places in this system, at the systemic risk regulator and then the day-to-day prudential regulators, the ability to say to any entity, 'you have to raise your capital, you're overextended'... (States News Service 2009)

Frank followed that up by chairing Congressional hearings during which TBTF was a major focus, ultimately leading to measures such as the Orderly Resolution Authority and new capital requirements rules, both targeted at the problem of TBTF.

Frank's counterpart, Republican Congressman Spencer Bachus, was the senior minority member on the House Financial Services Committee when Dodd-Frank was working its way through Congress. After the Republicans won control of the House, Bachus became the finance committee chair. In an interview with *Forbes* magazine in September

2009, he questioned the idea of the state dictating size limits for banks: "Do we want to limit the size of our corporations? From a global competitiveness [standpoint], I believe we need companies of the size that they can compete with some of the large European [firms] ..." (Wingfield 2009). Asked if that meant it might be necessary to allow for the existence of firms that might be considered TBTF, Bachus responded: "I wouldn't dismiss that. If you determine too big to fail then you're also saying too small to save, which is to me very unfair." In Congressional hearings following those comments, Bachus repeatedly emphasised that any solution should not involve regulatory entities being authorised to use taxpayer funds to rescue stricken firms, and he called for a provision that prohibited such funds being used (U.S. House Committee on Financial Services 2009b). He thus objected to the idea of the state trying to decide the appropriate size for institutions (A1) and the idea that it might use funds to respond to a bank failure (B1), both positions that are consistent with the market liberal Narrative 1.

The views of these political leaders were buttressed by the analysis offered by think tanks, according to where they landed on the ideological scale. For instance, the review of think tank publications noted earlier showed clear divisions among different think tanks for the two narratives. Cato and AEI, both right leaning, promoted positions in line with Narrative 1. The centrist Brookings, and to a lesser extent the National Bureau of Economic Research, offered an analysis that often aligned more with Narrative 2.

While Congressional leaders such as Frank and Bachus, and various think tanks, took positions that one might have expected based on their political parties or their ideological reputations, ultimately the question comes down to which narrative dominated political discourse. One clue may be found in the Congressional Record, which contains everything that is said on the floor of Congress. A search of the Congressional Record for the terms "too big to fail" and "bailout" over a five-year period showed a striking pattern (Table 4.3).

Table 4.3 TBTF and bailout references in Congress

Year	*"Too big to fail" references*	*"Bailout" references*
2008	27	300
2009	157	597
2010	303	360
2011	33	177
2012	25	101

In the immediate aftermath of 2008, the number of references to TBTF surged as legislators wrestled with the question of post-crisis regulation. But usage of the term collapsed in 2011, immediately after Republicans took over the House of Representatives. According to Narrative 1, broadly supported by the Republican caucus, the state should not take any action about TBTF, either in terms of prudential policy or limiting contagion. Consistent with the remarks from Bachus, a market liberal paradigm dismisses the concept of a firm being ever TBTF. In line with that stance, we see that a Republican-led House of Representatives simply ceased talking about it from 2011.

The degree to which TBTF was a major talking point in Congress during the 2009–2010 period, and then immediately ceased to be, thus can be seen as one indicator of Narrative 1 coming into the ascendency from 2011. Even when TBTF featured in Congressional hearings in the 2009–2010 period, a substantial amount of that debate involved political actors arguing that TBTF as a concept should not exist or highlighting the difficulty in defining what would be TBTF.[6]

The pattern reflects the intensity of regulatory discourse, which was naturally strongest in the 2009–2010 period when Dodd-Frank was being debated. A similar pattern can be seen with TBTF's sister term, "bailout." But there is a distinction. While the term "bailout" also was uttered less frequently after 2010, the decline was far less steep than was the case for TBTF. A narrative based on an interventionist paradigm needs to grapple with TBTF *and* with bailouts. A narrative based on a market liberal paradigm can dismiss or ignore TBTF but still talk about bailouts. Furthermore, the market liberal narrative links any discussion about bailouts to interventionism, not to bank behaviour or market failures. This is similar to narratives about crisis causes, where the interventionist narrative saw the financial industry as a chief cause, while the market liberal narrative focused on the role of government.

A review of who featured most often in Congressional committee testimony offers more hints about the emerging narrative. Between June 2009 and March 2012. Cato representatives testified 11 times before House and Senate finance committees, with all but two instances coming after the mid-term elections, when Republicans took control of the House. Appearances by representatives for Brookings decreased after the mid-terms. There were 13 examples of testimony during this period, with eight occurring when Democrats held both houses of Congress and five after the election. What is clear from this is that the prominence in Congressional debate of think tanks favouring one or the other narrative depended largely on what the political actors in power wanted to hear. Once voters elected more

Republicans to Congress, the prominence in Congressional debate of a think tank favouring Narrative 1 increased substantially.

Officials from the Financial Services Roundtable were also called in to testify before Congressional committees. On five occasions between June 2009 and March 2012 one of them spoke about TBTF. The organisation consistently questioned the validity of the concept. On 5 March 2009, Chief Executive Steve Bartlett testified:

> The definition of "systemic risk" should not be size based and thus, avoiding the too big to fail syndrome. Rather, systemic risk would be any risk to the broader system that can arise from the collective actions of hundreds or from significant actions of a few. (U.S. House Committee on Financial Services 2009a)

In testimony 12 days later, Bartlett said his group did not agree with the concept of too big to fail (U.S. House Committee on Financial Services 2009b). In October of that year, Roundtable official Scott Talbott added:

> We oppose the idea of "too-big-to-fail," and believe that if a firm is going to fail, it should be allowed to fail. Creative destruction is part of the market system. The key here is to strengthen the regulatory framework to spot developing trends, and then if the firm does fail, to minimize the effects of its demise on the entire system. (U.S. House Committee on Financial Services 2009c)

While the banking industry may have been highly unpopular at this time, the position the group took was in line with the public mood. Public polling between 2009 and 2012 suggested the issue of bailouts resonated with the public and that state policy was unpopular for an extended period. A January 2009 poll showed 61% of respondents opposed more money being provided for banks after an initial state cash infusion (CNN/Opinion Research Corporation 2009). The Harris Poll found 65% of respondents opposed bailouts for banks in 2009 and by 2012 a plurality (48% to 23%) believed it had been a mistake to bail them out (The Harris Poll 2012). One should not read too much into such polling results. But they show that Narrative 1, with its focus on banning bailouts, had appeal despite the aftermath of Lehman. The data suggest that Narrative 2, which is based on the need to prevent large bank failures, had not made as strong an impression.

How elite media wrote about TBTF

In the combined sample of *New York Times* and *Washington Post* articles, there were 38 stories that included the phrase "too big to fail," or nearly one in five. The sample included four *New York Times* and four *Washington Post* op-ed articles. Those pieces, written by economic authorities such as Paul Krugman or Simon Johnson, the former chief economist for the International Monetary Fund, presented evidence and built arguments in a logical fashion. The news articles, on the other hand, almost uniformly referred to the TBTF term as a problem but included little other information about it. A typical example, from the *Times* in February 2010, read: "John S. Reed, a former chairman of Citigroup, often mentioned as an example of an institution considered too big to fail, offered a different perspective" (Chan 2010). At first glance, even such barebones treatment of the term would appear to support an interventionist narrative since referring to TBTF institutions as a problem implies that a solution is needed. In such a reading, interventionism becomes the de facto policy paradigm.

All of this is in line with Narrative 2. Yet the ambiguity of the term TBTF and the lack of detail given when it was used also allowed for a Narrative 1 reading. In this interpretation, TBTF is the result of government interventionism, and the only fair and effective action would be the banning of bailouts. The conflation of the concept of TBTF with the deeply unpopular bailouts was arguably one of the more successful aspects of Narrative 1. It tapped into public frustration with all that the financial crisis represented. For readers primed to distrust state action after more than two decades of neoliberal policy discourse, references to TBTF thus could become associated with "unnecessary" state intervention. Such a reading relied on a convenient form of amnesia in terms of the perceived necessity of rescuing the financial system after the havoc of Lehman's collapse.

The more that "TBTF" and "bailout" become conflated within a market liberal narrative, the more that the problem facing society becomes "big government." TBTF has gone from being a crisis of capitalism to a crisis of interventionism. Along the way, a market liberal paradigm that had been blamed by some actors for being responsible for the crisis was able to be readopted as an emblem of a populist movement. Jules Boykoff and Eulalie Laschever (2011) write that Tea Party Movement activists attributed government bailouts as the catalyst for their initial protests. Matt Guardino and Dean Snyder (2012) also describe how corporate bailouts were seen by some Tea Party activists as evidence of a state-run "tax and spend" economy and they note an appeal to personal freedom by those opposed to interventionist policies.

> In the neoliberal worldview, the market ensures personal freedom; therefore, attempts at government regulation of economic decisions – whether in business, occupation, or consumption – impinge upon the freedom to choose. Accordingly, neoliberal discourse articulates a vision of government as an inefficient, cumbersome, overly bureaucratized entity prone to meddling in the private affairs of hardworking citizens, to the benefit of "undeserving" poor (minority) populations. (Guardino and Snyder 2012, p. 530)

In the absence of any information beyond the usage of TBTF as an adjective, a reading aligned with either narrative becomes possible. News media, in this sample, made no significant effort to investigate or explain the TBTF issue, despite including frequent references to it. This is not an unusual issue in media criticism. Scholars have long noted news media's propensity to reduce complex issues to shorthand, allowing nuances to get lost in the black-and-white language of news reporting. Nonetheless, here the dearth of nuanced, detailed reporting had the effect of producing something different from reductionism. It allowed for ambiguity.

To see how that ambiguity could favour a market liberal narrative, we can consider news media's treatment of the term "bailout." In the *New York Times* sample, the word "bailout" was used 82 times in 43 separate articles, meaning it came up in more than one third of the sample. This usage was substantially higher than that of the term TBTF, unsurprising given the public salience of bailouts. Characterisations of bailouts and bailout policy in the *New York Times* fell into six categories. Four of these could be considered bailout-critical:

1   Undeserving recipients: Bailouts benefited irresponsible and/or greedy firms
2   Innocent victims: Bailouts came at the cost of ordinary people (taxpayers)
3   Rigged system: Bailouts exemplified a corrupt system that featured cosy political relationships, a lack of accountability and moral hazard
4   Broad or undefined damage

A fifth category was bailout-positive, which highlighted the need for bailouts or benefits they offered. Finally, a sixth category was made up of neutral descriptions, such as factual references to bailouts with clinical language and little extraneous information. References to bailouts and policy overwhelmingly were in the bailout-critical categories. Of the 82 times the term appeared, there were only five instances where some kind of benefit or need for the bailouts was cited. In 21 cases, references to bailouts were neutral. In all other examples, one or more of the above four problem categories featured. For example, a 22 January 2010 article included the following:

> Yet even Mr. Geithner of late has been moving toward a tougher stance on Wall Street, in part out of anger that big banks, having ridden a taxpayer bailout back to comfortable profitability, are now rewarding themselves with big bonuses and fighting harder in Congress against the administration's initiative to tighten regulation of the financial system. (Calmes 2010a)

Banks are described here as "having ridden" the bailouts back to "comfortable profitability" before "rewarding themselves." These lexical choices suggest the banks gamed the system. The criticisms are syntactically presented as factual events. The account can be read as an argument for stronger interventionist policies to control the banks; but the reporting also characterises the state as an enabler of bad behaviour, which was one of the arguments of Narrative 1.

On 22 April 2010, in an article headlined "Bill on finance wins approval of Senate panel," the *Times* reported:

> Republicans expressed some confidence that they would eliminate that provision as well as the $50 billion fund, which supporters said was intended to ensure that taxpayers were not asked to finance future bailouts. Republicans have criticized it as "a bailout fund." (Wyatt and Herszenhorn 2010)

Whereas the first example was focused on the relationship between bailouts and banks (the "undeserving recipients" and the "rigged system" categories), this second example is focused on the impact on ordinary people (the "innocent victims" category). It should be noted that the *Times* report did include the important detail that the $50 billion fund was to be financed by banks and not the government. There is no indication that the *Times* reporters treated the term "bailout fund" as anything other than political spin, although they did repeat the term uncritically.

The "rigged system" category deserves particular attention. It considered bailouts as the result of regulatory capture whereby government and corporate accountability suffered (unlike the accountability achieved from a strict market-based system of reward and punishment). Here we see one of the market liberal arguments being made most clearly: That efforts to tighten regulation would lead to more bailouts.[7] The *New York Times* included a version of the regulation-will-perpetuate-bailouts line on at least 10 separate occasions. When the House of Representatives approved the Dodd-Frank bill, setting the stage for its enactment, a July 2010 report included this passage:

> House Republicans complained that the Democrats' legislation would extend the reach of government regulators too far, that it would encourage rather than prevent future bailouts, and that it would not address the causes of the financial crisis because it did not deal with the government-controlled mortgage giants, Fannie Mae and Freddie Mac. (Herszenhorn 2010)

Equally telling is what is missing: There is a dearth of references as to why the bailouts were undertaken in the first place, or the stabilising effect on the economy they may have had at a time of acute distress. A 20 August 2009 report referred to the bailouts as part of a list of "colossal rescue programs" (Andrews 2009); a 10 December 2009 article referred to "nonpartisan assessments" that the bailout programme was working, even if not as well as originally advertised (Calmes 2010b); the same report included commentary that credited the bailouts with preventing an economic panic; and finally, a 23 January 2011 report on Obama included a reference to his championing bailouts as practical (Baker 2011). Those references constitute the only instances when bailouts were presented as necessary or beneficial. While the *New York Times* is not obliged to repeatedly remind readers of the reason why bailouts were seen as needed in the chaotic months of late 2008, the dearth of such references can help explain the public amnesia referenced above.

The term bailout itself has a negative connotation in that it has come to imply potential malfeasance by the government as well as the firm requiring assistance. "Rescue" arguably is a term that has less of a negative connotation. The distinction was not lost on Republican presidential candidate John McCain amid efforts to secure capital for failing firms in the days after Lehman's collapse. "The first thing I would do is say, 'Let's not call it a bailout. Let's call it a rescue,'" McCain was quoted as saying (Public Broadcasting Service 2008).

McCain's plea did not appear to find a receptive audience within news media. A search of the *New York Times* sample found the word "rescue" or "rescues" turned up 12 articles and was used a total of 19 times. The term "bailout" was used more than four times as often.

The notion that future bailouts would be the result of a misguided state response to the crisis fit a broader pattern of framing regulation as a costly, economy-choking and unfair exercise. Many actors argued the bill, or aspects of it, would stifle innovation or make companies less competitive. The weaponisation of the page length of the Dodd-Frank Act, noted in Chapter 1, showed how pro-market actors sought to reinforce the pre-crisis paradigm by portraying the regulatory response as one of overreach. Banks would be hindered in their ability to make loans. Investment would be deterred. Capital would be driven out of the country. As former Texas Governor Rick Perry was quoted saying in one article: "It's the regulatory world that is killing America" (Fletcher 2011).

Consequence frames were the second most common type in the *Washington Post* sample, exceeded only by solution frames, as shown in Table 4.4. If we drill down to focus on consequence frames specifically, looking at both newspapers, a distinct picture emerges: Frames aligned with a market liberal paradigm outnumbered interventionist frames at a rate of more than two-to-one in the *Times* and nearly at that rate in the *Washington Post*. This is in sharp contrast to other frame types, where interventionist-aligned messages dominated.

Table 4.4 shows the total number of news frames from the *Washington Post* sample in five categories. The boxes highlighted indicate which frames dominated in each category. As discussed in Chapter 2, each sentence in each article was examined and coded based on the presence of frames grouped into different frame types.

When looking at the data over time, the dominance of market liberal framing becomes even clearer. As Dodd-Frank's passage approached, instances of market liberal framing increased, with political

Table 4.4 Consequence frame comparison

Washington Post frames	Problems	Causes	Solutions	Moral judgment	Consequences
Total	112	89	370	44	179
Interventionist	77	61	202	29	55
Market liberal	8	8	61	6	97
Unaligned	27	20	107	9	27

actors warning of the bill's consequences. These frames maintained a consistent advantage as the U.S. general election approached. The trend was highly similar at the two newspapers, indicating that this tendency was not limited to one newsroom culture.

Figure 4.1 shows the number of consequence frames in the combined *New York Times* and *Washington Post* sample from the introduction of the Dodd-Frank bill to end-March 2012.

But these charts only give an indication of the strength of the market liberal narrative. A closer inspection shows the underlying strength of its dominance. Each frame was grouped according to what messages were being presented, specifically based on whether the regulation would help or harm the (1) economy/broader public, (2) the business world or (3) the financial system.

Some of these "sub-frames" were extremely vague. When Former Texas Governor Perry spoke of the regulatory world "killing America," there was no specific consequence suggested but the message was broadly about the negative effects on the country. At the other end of the spectrum, when one newspaper source spoke of capital being driven out of the country, he pointed to a specific consequence for the system and the business community.

This close analysis of news media texts showed a heavy emphasis on market liberal sub-frames. They outnumbered interventionist sub-frames in all three categories. Sub-frames that focused on the economy and the public were the most common, accounting for nearly half of all

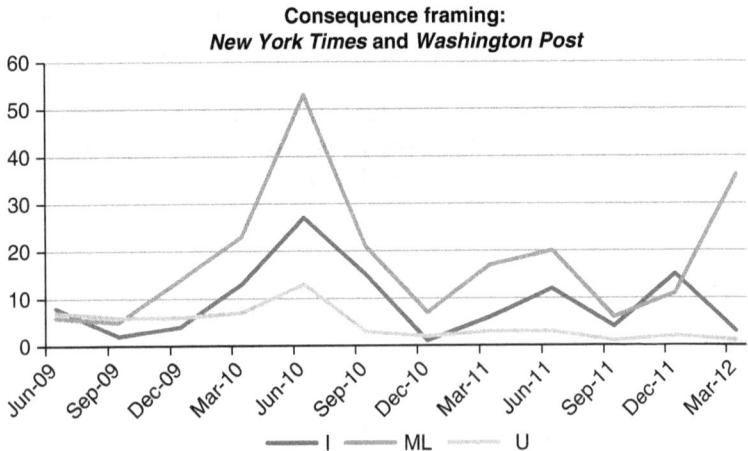

Figure 4.1 Consequence framing: *New York Times* and *Washington Post*.

the messages in the sample, while those that focused on the financial system were least common, with fewer than a quarter of the messages falling into that category.

A chief narrative strategy employed through sub-frames was to paint regulation as a job-killer. The most common sub-frames suggested regulation would reduce growth, investment and jobs, or would not address job concerns. There were 22 specific sub-frames talking about the harm from regulation to jobs, compared with just two that highlighted the way the regulation might protect jobs. Similarly, market liberal sub-frames that focused on the damage to businesses (via lower profits, lost competitiveness and increased red tape) outnumbered interventionist sub-frames about business by eight to one. In many cases, banks were portrayed as victims at the mercy of overzealous state actors.

State actors and journalists were the most common sources of consequence frames, accounting for three out of every four. Advocacy groups were the least represented actor group, accounting for only five frames in the entire sample. In fact, frames from financial industry actors outnumbered advocacy group frames by more than 10 to one (despite the industry shyness described in the preceding chapter).

Two findings stand out from the results. The first is that actors who promoted a market liberal paradigm focused on "pocketbook issues," namely those that affected people most directly. The second is that although Dodd-Frank was most concerned with systemic risk, that issue had far less resonance. The bulk of the framing treated financial policy regulation in an economic context, with political and corporate actors focusing on the impact interventionism would have on business activity, economic growth and jobs. To highlight one striking result, there were 120 frames in the sample that suggested regulation would hurt businesses, compared with 15 frames that suggested it would help businesses.

Taken together, the framing data reinforce a picture of government as intractably hostile to business, a notion that had long been advanced by actors such as Milton Friedman (Chapter 1). Despite the upheaval of the crisis, news media proved receptive to the market liberal Narrative 1 and to frames that focused on regulation's costs rather than its benefits. Whereas cause frames and moral judgment frames both leaned heavily towards interventionism, the pattern changed with consequence frames. When journalists, and the news sources they featured, spoke in terms of the consequences of regulation, more often than not it was unconnected to the events of the recent past. Even as the economic pain from the crisis was still being felt, an effort to shift the focus to the pain of regulation had begun and was proving successful.

The view from the newsroom

The *New York Times* and the *Washington Post* have long been accused, by right-wing politicians and their supporters, of having a left-of-centre bias. Some scholars have suggested the view is not baseless (c.f. Groseclose and Milyo 2005; Watts et al. 1999). But if that is the case, the framing data are all the more counterintuitive. Why would left-leaning news providers regularly frame issues in ways that reinforced a paradigm preferred by the right? Was there some stranglehold a market liberal paradigm had which led journalists to embrace such framing? Was there some factor linked to consequence framing?

The answer would not appear to relate to lack of awareness about agenda-building tactics. I asked Tom Braithwaite of the *Financial Times* whether it looked like an organised PR battle was being waged by groups such as the Financial Services Roundtable. "There certainly was a PR effort from certainly those lobby groups that you mentioned," he said. Another reporter who covered the banking industry for a prominent newspaper, and who asked for anonymity, saw a narrative emerging from Congressional committees and regulatory bodies such as the Commodity Futures Trading Commission (CFTC).

> There was definitely a lot of 'this financial overhaul will be too burdensome, and it won't go back to the root cause' discussion. I think that tended to be fairly predictable in terms of the less-regulation crowd and the Republicans.

Braithwaite saw a partisan divide in views about TBTF. "There were some big philosophical debates over too-big-to-fail that were quite prominent, which were largely Republican-Democratic in the split," he said. "I believe there was a genuine belief that institutions should be allowed to fail, and that Dodd-Frank was not helping that. It was the opposite."

Peter Thal Larsen, who at the time worked with Braithwaite at the *Financial Times*, said that as the crisis response became a political story, politicians responded by beating up on banks. "That was more or less the dynamic. 'We're going to crack down on these people,'" he said. Braithwaite, however, said that while Republican politicians may have talked tough, they still aligned themselves with financial industry interests. "Certainly, I think a lot of the Republican talking points were designed to appear critical of the industry – because big banks were no one's friends at the moment – while actually being entirely sympathetic to them and trying to further their interests," he said.

Such comments speak to a high level of agenda awareness. Faux banker-bashing may have been seen for what it was, but there were other tactics by pro-market actors that proved difficult to guard against. One involved perpetuating false narratives about how finance works. Another was for actors to focus on pocketbook issues, knowing that these would resonate and thus capitalising on journalists' news values. Meanwhile, reporters responded with their own efforts to avoid being spun. As a rule, journalists dislike the idea they may be tools to further someone's agenda.

False narratives and pocketbook issues

As part of the market liberal narrative concerning TBTF, an argument was made that measures to address banks' systemic implications would harm the economy. Large banks, it was argued, would have to reserve more capital as a percentage of their assets. In banking, loans that have been made are assets; capital requirements thus measure how much capital a bank has compared with its lending. Those opposed to tougher regulation argued that higher capital requirements would result in lower lending.

Enrich of the *New York Times* said this narrative about capital requirements had become widely accepted in news media simply because it seemed intuitive. But he said it was unsupported by any academic research he could find.

> It is just demonstrably true that this false narrative took hold in the media, fuelled by politicians and regulators but mostly by the banks, that the higher capital requirements are, the less banks will lend and therefore there's this clear dampening effect on economic growth.

Enrich, working then at the *Wall Street Journal*, said he wrote a story about how this misconception about finance had become gospel: "It occurred to me ... 'Wait, this is not how capitalism works, there's no reason that the argument for saying that this hurts the economy had become the accepted truth of the matter. It's not true.'" He spoke about the issue to Charles Dallara, who was head of a lobby group called the Institute for International Finance. Dallara, he said, acknowledged there might not be research to support the idea that higher capital requirements would curb lending, but said it stood to reason that they would.

> I'm like, are you kidding me? Like, this was just like the word of God for journalists that ... the higher capital requirements go, the lower the lending goes. We just accepted that.

Carter Dougherty, who worked at Bloomberg from 2010 to 2016 and covered the consumer protection beat, described a variant on this narrative. He recalled an instance when a source complained that Dodd-Frank would limit financial sector activity.

> I did have this conversation with a bank lobbyist one time, and I said, like, arguably that's a good thing, because finance is supposed to be an intermediary in an economy. It wrangles savings for productive uses in the so-called real economy. So, to the extent that there is less money being made in finance, that means that a greater chunk of it is going to productive economic activity and not, you know, not financial intermediation.

Dougherty, who left the news agency to work for Americans for Financial Reform, said he had to roll his eyes at times. "This is the sort of argument that you hear with virtually any regulation in any sector, that this will result in a less dynamic economy." He treated such comments as "a reflex, not an argument" and did not always feel the need to include them in his articles. Still, the anecdotes from Enrich and Dougherty are examples where journalists spotted the logical flaw in a narrative and were able to push back. The question here is whether that was the exception or the rule.

The capital-requirements-equals-lower-lending line was one of many sub-narratives that fell within the "pocketbook issues" theme in the framing. Another issue was bailouts, and here one interviewee drew a direct connection between a media narrative and state policy. Bailouts became a pocketbook issue because the market liberal narrative – in focusing on the taxes paid by citizens – connected the notion of corporate rescues with personal finances. Dodd-Frank did not ban bailouts but, in response to the strength of the anti-bailout discourse, Title XIII of the law set limits on the use of public funds for bailouts in future. Diana B. Henriques, a Pulitzer Prize finalist who wrote about regulation for the *New York Times,* said the media's acceptance of the bailout narrative was a factor in that decision.

> One of the worst aspects of the Dodd-Frank legislation was its hostility toward bailouts. This was one of the places where a different perspective, a better historical perspective, by the financial media might have made an enormous difference. The rhetoric and coverage of financial bailouts in the lead-up to the enactment of Dodd-Frank led to the inclusion in that bill of what I believe is a ticking time bomb.

The time bomb she envisioned was created by the language in Dodd-Frank that would make it more difficult to conduct a bailout in future. She placed some blame on the government's own failure to do more to prevent homeowner foreclosures, which fed a separate narrative that the state was more concerned with helping Wall Street than ordinary people. "That frame around the issue of rescuing a failing financial institution is with us to this day. It is so ahistorical, it is so ignorant about what competent regulators will be required to do to save the financial system in the midst of a future crisis, it just drives me crazy," Henriques said.

By focusing on pocketbook issues, actors were trafficking in topics that resonated with the public, increasing the likelihood that such framing would make it into stories. Ledyard King, a correspondent with Gannett, said:

> I think we focused on the issues that most of our readers we felt would know about, would be hurt most, be affected most. And in many cases, reporters are much like – at least reporters here – are much like our readers. You know, we have 401(k)s, we have mortgages, we have car loans, we want prices to stay low and our investments to go up. There was no sort of directive to write it like that. I just think it's how we did, how we understood it, what we needed to do and that was it.[8]

The pocketbook theme that Henriques and King noted highlights the way that agenda-building actors understand a core aspect of media production, namely the concept of news values. Johan Galtung and Mari Holmboe Ruge in 1965 identified a tendency by journalists to make coverage decisions based on a consistent set of factors (Galtung and Ruge 1965). Their study was updated by Tony Harcup and Deirdre O'Neill, who suggested that audience relevance should be seen as a leading news value (Harcup and O'Neill 2001).

The journalistic response

Journalists often rely on a default posture of scepticism to prevent sources from pushing an agenda. David Herszenhorn of Politico said reporters for major news providers almost automatically fight against efforts to sell a claim about the future without it being grounded.

> Our instinct as reporters is there, to never let somebody get away with making a bold pronouncement, a promise to voters or

constituents that we don't then fact check and truth-patrol, right in the moment ... This was something we just did on Capitol Hill as a matter of standard operating procedure. If somebody says this is going to do X, Y or Z, we would say, you know, maybe it will, maybe it won't, based on whatever we knew at the moment to be, you know, the factual grounding for that.

Francesco Guerrera, who was at the *Financial Times*, made a similar point. He said most journalists were trained to "discount any sort of categorical statement, and immediately, almost Pavlovianly, look for the other side." He said this practice was especially ingrained in American media.

Brian Tumulty, who worked for Gannett during the crisis aftermath, said there was a legitimate debate to be had about how much to regulate and how to regulate. But he also recognised the traps that some sources might lay.

I'm fairly familiar with the topic and have a master's degree in economics, so I'm not an unsophisticated journalist, just regurgitating what was said, you know, or leading readers down dead-end debates. I tried to focus on what was the real issue of the day and that you know kind of guided me. And what were they, you know, truly disagreeing about. You know, what was the nub of the issue? I don't know how well I did that, but that was my goal.

Several journalists spoke of their efforts to ensure they understood the subject matter deeply. Caren Bohan, who covered Dodd-Frank for Reuters and now is with *USA Today*, described her research with regards to the Volcker Plan debate: "I tried to intellectually understand both sides of it. I tried to, you know, learn as much as I could about the arguments on each side and where Volcker was coming from in making sure that nothing like this ever happened again." Kevin Hall of McClatchy read works such as *This Time Is Different*, a historical analysis of financial crises by Reinhart and Rogoff (2009). "That had a big influence in terms of how I approached my reporting, trying to think about ways in which, you know, what would come back first, what's going to take longer to come back," he said.

Enrich, whose initial scepticism led to him challenging the conventional wisdom about capital requirements, got help from some of the sources he came to trust. He referenced Sheila Bair, who was then leading the Federal Deposit Insurance Corporation, and Anat Admati, an academic who had highlighted the issue in critiques of the banking industry. Such help was needed. "I think probably 95% of the financial media did not fundamentally understand how a bank balance sheet works," Enrich said.

Journalists whose beat focused on finance or who had a background in economics – such as Dougherty, Tumulty, Herszenhorn, Hall and Enrich – thus felt able to challenge claims made by sources or at least not accept them wholesale. But many journalists, such as general assignment reporters, do not encounter such lightbulb moments or receive the benefit of careful explanations from senior regulators or academics. Ledyard King of Gannett recalled the question of bailouts during the immediate crisis management phase:

> Someone with my background, or lack of background, I didn't know enough to be able to say they were wrong, or they were right. For most of the coverage we try to explain in simple terms, maybe too simple ... You had Bush and Obama essentially agreeing on a bailout package. That, to my untrained mind at least, it was something where at least where there's bipartisan agreement on something as major as this.

For a beat reporter, gaining a deep understanding of an issue could pay dividends. For a reporter who dipped into the Dodd-Frank story occasionally, it had less value. King's experience – to the extent that it was shared by other journalists at the time – highlights the vulnerability some reporters felt when dealing with the myriad technical issues that the regulatory story encompassed.

Another response was for reporters to talk to as many sources as possible, just as they did when dealing with cause framing. This was the case even for journalists who had covered financial regulation for years. Stephen Labaton said of his time with the *New York Times* that dealing with consequence arguments went with the territory of writing about regulation.

> Every major piece of legislation and regulation involves an attempt at predicting how that rule or law or regulation will alter conduct in a way, either harmful or beneficial. Journalists who are used to hearing the parade of horribles from people, and you're used to also hearing the ... advocated benefits of it, I think the challenge is to try to ground it in some reality in all cases.

Labaton aimed to reflect a wide array of views in his articles, recognising that *New York Times* readers were a sophisticated audience, but also "to try to do some truth-squadding where one can and to try to call out bullshit when it was bullshit where you could." He noted: "You're dealing with financial institutions; you're dealing with regulatory bodies – all have their own agendas." Herszenhorn, meanwhile, said one tactic was to find people who thought about issues but "don't necessarily have a dog in the fight."

The steps these journalists took – starting from a position of scepticism, trying to educate themselves and speaking to a wide range of sources – are the sort of standard operating procedures that are taught in journalism schools and routinely advised by veteran reporters when covering difficult-to-understand, complex stories. They are designed to prevent one side of a story from getting undue weight or false narratives from being perpetuated. As elite media journalists, these reporters would be expected to follow such procedures, and by their accounts they did. Yet, one side of the story did appear to get extra weight and false narratives did appear to make it into news pages. What, then, might explain this?

The challenge of truth-squadding

The media scholar Jay Rosen, in writing about "he-said-she-said" journalism (2009), voiced frustration with situations where there was a newsworthy public dispute but no serious attempt to assess clashing truth claims. I interviewed Simon Denyer, who was Washington bureau chief for Reuters when Dodd-Frank was being debated, and asked about this. He described a kind of "atomisation of news," whereby incremental breaking news lent itself to people making claims about the future and their acceptance, without journalists stepping back to take a big picture view.

Another problem with consequence frames, however, comes from the weak-feedback mechanism issue that Jerit cited in her analysis of politicians' predictive appeals. As Labaton said of one set of clashing predictions he encountered during the repeal of Glass-Steagall story: "One would definitively never know until it either happened or never happened."

There were epistemological considerations as well. In the cases where Labaton and Herszenhorn spoke about truth-squadding, they appeared to be referring to cases of specific predictions. But as the content analysis showed, many of the consequence frames were vague. Experienced political actors understand the attraction of media-friendly sound bites, particularly if they are vague. For the journalist, there may be news value from including them, while there is little incentive to try to debunk them since such discussions risk descending into a philosophical debate (which is generally not the stuff of news reports). In the realm of consequence framing, then, vague statements stand a better chance of being included despite the "truth-squadding" function journalists may try to perform.

Yet while the discussion above explains the difficulty in dealing with consequence frames in general, it does not account for why the balance of such frames in the sample was so decidedly in favour of the market liberal paradigm. The answer would appear to be based on a combination of media production factors, from the skill and sophistication of agenda-builders to the loss of institutional memory in newsrooms.

Enrich, for instance, suggested certain narratives catch on easily because the actors promoting them are adept. "Well-financed interest groups and lobby organisations are very good at assembling anecdotes and examples and, like, find the farmer who couldn't like get a loan to buy his new tractor because his bank has a ton of capital requirements," he said.

Herszenhorn also noted that journalists could have unconscious agendas. He said the backgrounds, educations and personal histories of the editors and the colleagues he worked with meant they saw the world in different ways, and that meant they would see news stories in different ways. Journalists at the *Times*, he added, will not reflect the diversity of readers, many of whom have never owned shares.

> They write about it (the regulatory story) from the perspective of people who have something to win or lose based on the performance of the stock market. You know, that alone predisposes you to a certain bias that you can't forget, right? You can't forget that you have money in the bank or that you have money in your mutual fund or you have money in your 401(k) .... . There are people ... at the *New York Times* who can't imagine living anywhere but the Upper West Side of Manhattan, right? And that will shape your worldview.

In this respect, the focus on pocketbook issues potentially becomes even more effective. In appealing not only to what journalists think their readers might care about but also to what the journalists themselves care about, actors have a greater chance of getting their frames and narratives adopted.

Another issue Enrich highlighted is that the journalism industry is constantly losing institutional memory, making it less equipped to combat efforts to advance a narrative based on a false premise.

If you are a 25-year-old journalist, you know, with no business or banking or financial experience – so basically what I was 15 or 20 years ago – you have no capacity to kind of challenge that narrative or to really understand the fundamentals of what you're writing about in a way that will allow you to reach your own conclusions without relying on this accepted wisdom that's spread by the banks, or by the regulators who are right now at least in the banks' pockets.

Enrich described this factor as a "huge handicap" that is fundamental to the way that journalism operates because there are always going to be younger people coming into beats with less experience. "And more often than not they are going to get snowed."

Henriques, in her critique of the media for accepting the bailout narrative, connected the issue of the loss of institutional memory with the emotional appeal of pocketbook framing.

It is a fact that too many people in the financial media have little or no knowledge of financial history … . They didn't know how 1987 unfolded, and therefore they couldn't use that as a template to calculate the disaster that would have occurred if Dodd-Frank had been in effect in 1987.

Guerrera also highlighted the institutional memory issue. "Now it's a new generation of reporters who don't remember Dodd-Frank, or the reasons why Dodd-Frank came into place," he said. Asked whether institutional memory could fade that quickly in the news business, he said: "I think so. I was talking to a colleague of mine the other day and I was casually mentioning Dick Fuld – and he's 30? – and he had no idea who I was taking about."

Richard Fuld was the chairman and chief executive officer of Lehman Brothers when it filed for bankruptcy protection on 15 September 2008.

Notes

1 The search generated 115 publications. Of those, 42 papers were omitted because they were not focused on financial regulation or were not examples of original research (e.g., a reprint of an article from elsewhere).
2 Gary Dymski says C.V. Conover, a regulator, used the phrase. My own review of the 655-page hearing transcript did not show Conover using it, although at one point he responded to a question as to whether institutions of

certain sizes "simply are not allowed to fail or cannot be allowed to fail" (U.S. House Committee on Banking, Finance and Urban Affairs 1984, p. 292).

3 Evidence of the term's resonance with the public can be seen from the success of *Too Big to Fail: The Inside Story of How Wall Street and Washington Fought to Save the Financial System – and Themselves* (Sorkin 2009), which was later made into a movie.

4 The unfairness of the problem was neatly captured by the notion that the government was "privatising profits and socialising losses." Variants of that phrase had been used before the crisis, though it gained currency in the aftermath, with news media using it as well as prominent economists such as Joseph Stiglitz (CNBC 2010).

5 The Overton Window was developed by Joseph Overton in the mid-1990s (Mackinac Center for Public Policy 2020; Russell 2006). It takes any policy issue and places all conceivable options along a spectrum. At the outer edges of the spectrum, options might be considered unthinkable. Further in, they might be deemed radical. As one moves towards the centre from either end, options may be thought of acceptable, sensible or popular. The window concept holds that for a policy option to become viable, it must be within a range from "acceptable" to "popular." If not, public opinion needs to change until the option falls within that window.

6 Examples of this could be seen in a 29 October 2009 hearing that focused on TBTF (U.S. House Committee on Financial Services 2009c).

7 Anti-statist arguments are often based on the concept of "unanticipated consequences" (Merton 1936). The idea, commonly referred to as "unintended consequences," is associated with an argument that the state lacks the knowledge to foresee the damage its policies might cause.

8 A 401(k) is a personal pension plan (*Retirement Topics – 401(k) and Profit-Sharing Plan Contribution Limits* 2020).

5 An absent debate: The intersection of high finance and morality

News media, as the framing analysis has shown, regularly wrote about the factors that led to the crisis, the problems policymakers faced and the consequences of proposed solutions. Given the scale of the damage and the backdrop of widening income inequality, the discussion often took on a moral dimension within public debate. Which actors were morally culpable? Who were the biggest victims? How did moral transgressions take place? These all became questions that could inject drama for a conflict-hungry news media industry reporting on an otherwise dry and technical subject.

The frame category of "moral judgment," as employed by Robert Entman (1993), is used here to understand the degree to which morality-focused frames featured in regulatory coverage when compared with other frame types. This chapter considers which issues prompted discussion from a moral perspective and which actors were given media space to voice their moral judgments. Even though morality was a central issue in public debate about the crisis, moral framing within the coverage of the regulatory response was far less common than any other kind of framing.

The chapter begins with a brief discussion about how linkages between morality and finance have featured in both popular culture and academic literature. It will then examine Dodd-Frank coverage from the news media sample, identifying trends in the types of moral frames employed and how they were aligned with policy paradigms. As with other chapters, the final section will feature views from journalists who covered the story in order to understand why morality was so rarely used to frame issues, and what implications stemmed from the absence of such framing.

When journalists covering the Dodd-Frank story did frame matters in terms of morality, their texts were mostly aligned with an interventionist paradigm. Such framing, however, was sporadic. Many

DOI: 10.4324/9781003177944-5

journalists felt a professional duty to avoid writing about regulation in terms of what might be conceived of "right" or "wrong." Whatever moral indignation they or their sources might have felt did not infuse the coverage.

Markets and morality: A long tradition

News media's role in defining moral norms, particularly since the publication of sociologist Stanley Cohen's *Folk Devils and Moral Panics* (1973), has often been thought of in terms of social deviance. Highly visible challenges to the societal status quo become moral transgressions, making for easy news copy. As Cohen observes,

> The media have long operated as agents of moral indignation in their own right: Even if they are not self-consciously engaged in crusading or muck-raking, their very reporting of certain 'facts' can be sufficient to generate concern, anxiety, indignation or panic. (Cohen 1973, p. 16)

The main actors in the financial crisis, however, represented a different kind of moral threat, one marked by social convention rather than deviance. Unlike the "mods" and "rockers" in Cohen's analysis of 1960s Britain, the alleged villains of 2008 had *appeared* to play by the rules. That only made their behaviour all the more damning. News media depicted "greedy bankers" and "fat cats" who sought to play by a different set of rules than the rest of society.

There is a long tradition of depicting financial figures negatively in moral terms within popular Western culture. This tradition provides a set of reference points for society (and specifically for journalists) whenever the salience of financial matters is higher than normal. Fictional characters who have dominated the popular imagination, from Shakespeare's Shylock to Dickens's Scrooge, have led to the marketplace broadly being equated with avarice.

In the 20th century, many of the most striking moral characterisations of the world of finance have coincided with periods of extremes, either during times of plenty such as in the 1920s and 1980s, or times of scarcity, such as the 1930s. During times of plenty, the moral focus was on the self-interested "Homo economicus" (Mill 1844) who engaged in excessive consumption. We can see this from the titular character in F. Scott Fitzgerald's *The Great Gatsby* (Fitzgerald 1925) to Oliver Stone's film *Wall Street* (Stone and Pressman 1987). Market-led booms and dubious morality went hand in hand as the allure of lavish lifestyles threatened to undermine the moral fibre of the nation. During times of scarcity, the moral lens in the United States was focused more on the corrosive effects of raw power. We see this in the work of director Frank Capra, as he shows "big business" to be morally bankrupt in its oppression of the "little guy." Bankers act as corrupt agents who help greedy people and companies accrue more power. Fictional villains in both cases were ready to create their own morality to justify the systems that rewarded them. This is the basis for financier Gordon Gekko's much-cited "greed is good" speech in *Wall Street*. Gekko has many spiritual ancestors, notably the fictional banker Henry F. Potter in *It's a Wonderful Life* (Capra 1946). These fictional characters represent the cold, morality-free logic of the marketplace and the notion that might makes right.

Interventionism, however, is hardly seen as the automatic answer to moral questions, at least by those who have advocated a market liberal paradigm. For instance, James M. Buchanan, a Nobel Prize-winning economist and former Mont Pèlerin Society president, in writing about the relationship between the market, the state and morality, called for institutional reform that considered "man's moral limitations" (Buchanan 1978, p. 364) while still arguing for a reduced role by the state. In Buchanan's account, a strong, centralised state erodes morality because it encourages self-interested behaviour. His solution to preserve both economic competition and morality was the devolution of state power. In absence of such reform, the state remains vulnerable to regulatory capture: Buchanan warns of the "increasing resort to the power of the national government by those persons and groups who seek private profit" (Buchanan 1978, p. 368).

As might be expected, the post-crisis think-tank literature on the regulatory challenges makes little direct mention of morality, apart from scattered references to "bad" behaviour. But while the idea of morality itself may not feature prominently in think tank papers, moral considerations underpinned many of the issues that the authors analysed. Often this took place through the connection of moral hazard, systemic incentives and systemic risk. The concept of moral hazard originated from the insurance industry; it relates to morality in the sense that insurers were concerned that having insurance could induce people to become more reckless than they otherwise might be.

One of the clearest examples of a moral issue stemming from systemic incentives was the amount of money bankers made. The extent to which bankers' pay rewarded short-termism and excessive risk-taking was a systemic issue. But the high salaries and bonuses that were paid to Wall Street bankers, in the context of the financial crisis, could also be viewed easily through a moral lens. Similarly, a matter as technical as capital requirements could be thought of in moral terms due to the relationship between capital cushions and what, in hindsight, was deemed to be reckless behaviour by financial executives. Even the lack of reliable information about risks and exposures, with which banks and regulators could have made more sensible decisions, had a moral dimension. This lack of information offers a partial explanation for why executives behaved as they did; but in light of the severe effects that those decisions had on society, such a "we didn't see it coming" argument left both the financial services industry and the state open to charges of moral culpability, at least by critics of modern capitalism.

Within the broad theme of systemic incentives, the specific issue of remuneration received limited attention in the think tank literature. It was discussed at length in one instance, which was a summary of testimony by Brookings Senior Fellow Martin Baily to the House Financial Services Committee. Of the think tanks reviewed here, Brookings was most explicitly in favour of Dodd-Frank and its aims, with authors often offering analysis or proposals that called for the state to take some action to limit financial services firms from engaging in excessively risky behaviour. Baily, for instance, argued that the state had a legitimate interest in setting rules for compensation, although he said officials should not seek to regulate the actual level of pay. He noted that traders and CEOs were often rewarded on the basis of short-term profits, encouraging them to take risks that may have paid well in the short run, but which lost large sums in the long run. "One element of a more stable financial system involves compensation structures for those in financial institutions that do not incent excessive risk taking" (Baily 2010).

Baily appeared before Congress as a member of a group of economists with academic, private sector and public policy experience known as the Squam Lake Group. The group, which formed in late 2008 to discuss policymaking in light of the crisis, published a report in 2010 that received attention from lawmakers. But this is not to say that Baily, or others in the think tank community, were focused on morality itself. In a popular debate that began decades before the financial crisis, many actors have argued that it is not possible to "legislate morality." This idea had been countered – in one case famously by Dr Martin Luther King Jr – by the argument that it was still possible to pass laws that discouraged people from committing immoral acts. But the debate highlights the problem of any legislation or rulemaking that involves understanding factors such as personal intent. Indeed, another Brookings fellow, Douglas Elliott, when critiquing the Volcker

Rule on proprietary trading in 2012 testimony, noted that the rule rested on subjective distinctions. Operationalising it, he said, "forces regulators to peer into the hearts of bankers, which will prove to be extremely difficult, if not impossible" (Elliott 2012).

Still, the crisis did prompt some academic researchers to consider moral questions directly. David Weitzner and James Darroch (2009) sought to determine whether moral concepts such as hubris and greed could be linked with crises; they found that the development of a shadow banking system and opaque products were motivated in part by greed, and they used their findings to argue for regulatory solutions that increased transparency.

A number of researchers, beyond those in the think tank sample, also focused on executive pay, although several of these studies downplayed the notion that banker remuneration trends posed societal risks, or that new regulatory solutions were needed. Paul Gregg, Sarah Jewell and Ian Tonks (2012) concluded that it was unlikely that incentive structures induced the focus on the short term in financial services. John Core and Wayne Guay (2010) had reservations about proposals to regulate executive pay in financial services. Hamid Mehran, Alan D. Morrison and Joel D. Shapiro (2011), in a paper for the New York Federal Reserve, noted that bank regulators have an economic argument for controlling executive pay since the national deposit insurance system contributes to the size of a financial services firm, and size and executive pay are highly correlated. They proposed linking bankers' compensation to credit default swap spreads to address a perceived moral hazard. Tung (2011) also proposed structural changes in banker remuneration to ameliorate the "gambler's incentive" that caused firms to take risks at the expense of creditors and others.

Consensus, from this limited sample, was lacking about both the nature of moral hazard or the appropriate solutions, with some proposing a more interventionist approach and others, conversely, calling for the avoidance of more state involvement. While a consensus remained elusive on "legislating morality" for the financial industry, the academic community at least responded to the crisis by seeking to consider ways in which immoral behaviour or incentives could be identified and addressed. But as will be seen in the next section, elite news media showed little interest in the moral dimensions of the regulatory story, either in terms of outrage or incentives.

The elusive moral frame

Examples of framing involving moral judgment frames were the rarest in the *Washington Post* sample, accounting for less than 5% of the total number of frames that were coded. That does not mean post-crisis coverage did not focus on issues that had moral dimensions. A Nexis search of the *Post* coverage during the same time period generated 352 articles that dealt with executive pay, which was among the most prevalent topics that came up whenever morality was discussed.[1] Rather, the framing analysis suggests that coverage of the regulatory debate itself, in terms of moral framing, appeared to be limited. This is still mildly surprising given decades of research related to news values (Galtung and Ruge 1965; Harcup and O'Neill 2001) and the obvious appeal of highlighting moral culpability for its dramatic qualities.

Table 5.1 shows the total number of frames from the *Washington Post* sample for five frame categories. As discussed in Chapter 2, each sentence in each article was examined and coded based on the presence of frames grouped into different frame types.

The limited nature of moral discussion is confirmed by the number of articles in which these frames appeared. For instance, moral judgment frames appeared at least once in nearly three out of every 10 articles in the sample. Consequence frames, by comparison, were twice as common, appearing in more than six out of every 10 articles. In other words, it was much more likely that someone, when reading an article about Dodd-Frank, would hear about the economic consequences of regulation than about issues of morality. Both frame types were given similar prominence within stories. On average, a moral judgment frame appeared in the 11th paragraph of an article, the same as the average for consequence frames.

We can see from Table 5.1 that when issues were framed in moral terms, it tended to have an interventionist alignment. Such framing fell into three main categories. Firstly, there were frames about injustice with regard to the powerful, discussing them in terms of the harm they caused or special treatment they received. Secondly, there were frames about victims. Often these were ordinary people, frequently referred to as taxpayers and thus emphasising the unfairness of the situation at

Table 5.1 Moral judgment frame comparison

Washington Post frames	*Problem*	*Cause*	*Solution*	*Moral judgment*	*Consequence*
Interventionist	77	62	202	29	55
Market liberal	8	8	61	6	97
Unaligned	27	19	107	9	27
Totals	**112**	**89**	**370**	**44**	**179**

Totals in Table 5.1 show the number of frames in each category based on the research methodology (Chapter 2).

hand because they themselves were funding clean-up efforts. The very use of the term "taxpayer" thus has a moral quality. Victims also could be small companies caught up in the regulatory overhaul, or firms that were said to be blameless, such as community banks (of the type portrayed in Capra's *It's a Wonderful Life*). Thirdly, there was "the system," the structural forces and arrangements that allowed moral transgressions to occur; this included frames about lack of accountability. Some frames, such as those that talked about "Wall Street versus Main Street" and how powerful banks were walking all over ordinary people, could involve two or all three of these categories.

Discussion about executive pay was often categorised as moral judgment framing due to the way it referenced public outrage. Just before the Dodd-Frank bill was first unveiled, for instance, one article had focused on how punitive the Obama administration should be with financial firms. The reporters wrote: "Officials are seeking to address widespread anger over lavish Wall Street pay without discouraging firms from participating in the government's financial rescue programs" (Cho and Appelbaum 2009). A few days later, a similar reference was made: "The initiative reflects public uproar over executive compensation, which has been stoked by the financial crisis" (Cho, Goldfarb and Tse 2009). The policy decision-making here is being framed in terms of moral outrage, which has become a central factor in the policy process. The public, one could say, has a virtual seat at the policy-making table and the journalists are noting that it wants morality to be taken into account.

Public anger escalated when it was learned that the same financial firms that had taken cash infusions from the government months earlier had also earmarked some of those funds for bonuses. The *Washington Post* wrote: "The increase in set-asides for employee pay has raised the ire of Washington, where lawmakers denounced financial leaders for returning to old habits and vowed to enact measures governing executive compensation" (Tse 2009). House Financial Services Committee Chairman Barney Frank was quoted calling the amounts "troubling." In the same article, President Obama complained about the lack of remorse on the part of the bankers: "With respect to compensation, I'd like to think that people would feel a little remorse and feel embarrassed and would not get million-dollar or multimillion-dollar bonuses," he said (Tse 2009).

The bankers here are framed – by the political leaders being quoted – as morally culpable on at least three levels: for acting irresponsibly in the first place, for failing to see the error of their ways as they continued to display greed, and for compounding the misery of the taxpaying public by adding insult to injury. Finally, bankers were morally condemned for attempting to avoid accountability. Obama, in a March 2010 article, was quoted saying: "We will stand firm against any attempt by the financial sector to avoid their responsibilities: In any future crisis, the big financial companies must pay, not taxpayers" (Dennis 2010b).

Journalists were not short of sources who were eager to characterise bankers as greedy and reckless, although they tended to stick to political sources in their regulation-related coverage. In one of the rare occasions when the articles in the sample cited public advocacy campaigners, the moral framing took this approach and was one of the few frames to display raw emotion (evidenced by the verb "ravaged" and the reference to personal harms):

> But Ed Mierzwinski of the U.S. Public Interest Research Group, a leading consumer advocate, applauded the measure. "It's been over a year and a half since taxpayers bailed out the Wall Street bankers after their reckless actions ravaged our economy and cost us our jobs, our retirement income and our homes," he said. (Cho and Dennis 2010b)

The most common frames were of the Wall Street/Main Street variety, with 13 instances where this juxtaposition was used in moral terms. Some of these frames had a distinctively Hollywood quality to them. On 11 February 2010, in an article about growing support for a consumer protection agency, one political figure who was quoted is practically channelling the lead character from Capra's *Mr. Smith Goes to Washington* (Capra 1939):

> "This is a classic choice that members of Congress and the Senate have," Iowa Attorney General Tom Miller said on a call Tuesday, speaking along with several other state attorneys general in support of the new consumer agency. "Senators have to ask themselves: 'Whose side am I on? Am I on the side of the public, or am I on the side of big banks?'" (Dennis 2010a)

Drama was also heightened when Wall Street/Main Street frames focused on personalities. Elizabeth Warren was one of the most notable people in this respect as some actors sought to portray her in Hollywood-style heroic terms, as someone with grassroots support who stood up to the powerful. In a 20 July 2010 article, Americans for Financial Reform Director Heather Booth praised Warren for her "steadfast and tireless commitment to protecting consumers" (Dennis 2010d). Booth's language frames Warren and her mission in moral terms, evoking a Sisyphean struggle against forces that seek to exploit the masses. The term "consumer protection" itself has a moral dimension in that it speaks to the need to *protect* ordinary people from predatory corporations. Of course, political actors are well-versed in the utility of naming bills and agencies in such terms, and advocacy campaigners are equally well-versed in how to tap into feelings about morality as they frame issues in news media.

Corporate bailouts were discussed extensively in the sample, although those were only framed explicitly in moral terms seven times. The subject of executive compensation similarly came up regularly, although it was framed in direct moral terms only six times; more often it was framed as a contributing cause of the crisis, but without a moral context. Another issue was negligence, in terms of officials not doing their jobs properly (six moral fames). This theme of negligence also came up in terms of the powerful (four times) as well as borrowers (twice). Other frames in the sample included calls for banks to pay their "fair share" (Dennis and Murray 2010) and to be "held accountable" (Merle 2010), and for lawmakers to fix loopholes that Wall Street firms could exploit (Cho 2010).

There were only six distinct times in the sample when an actor framed something in terms that suggested that a market liberal policy approach offered the morally superior path. One case involved indignation that the government might rescue some borrowers when others had behaved responsibly. A few other frames were focused on the perceived immorality of government interventionism. On the eve of the bill's passage, for instance, the *Washington Post* reported on final negotiations over sticking points as Democrats sought to secure Republican backing in order for the bill to have bipartisan support. The article cited banking lobbyists who were upset about a proposed bank fee which they said would unfairly penalise banks that were blameless (Yang 2010). Framing regulatory efforts to rein in Wall Street as unfair in this way is in line with the idea that the state will inevitably be ham-fisted, a core argument made by those advocating market liberal policy positions.

It is important to note that these are just handfuls of frames, and they occur in a pool of nearly 1,000 frames over an extended period in the *Post* sample. The point here of considering how often these frames occurred is to highlight the opportunities for certain types of frames in order to see the avenues that journalists – or their sources – did *not* take, as much as those that they did. In opting for consequence frames more than four times as often as moral judgment frames, were journalists signaling a collective sense of the importance of economic impact as opposed to moral justice? Or were journalists simply dealing with the cards they were dealt as other actors chose the frames that suited their strategies? There is no definitive answer, although the responses from interviews suggest a mixture of both.

Do the right thing: Morality and paradigms

The underlying message with the moral frames in the sample was that wrongs had been committed and that the state should do something about them. This is consistent with a more interventionist approach, one that is in contrast to what had been seen before the financial crisis, when consensus held that a self-correcting market should be employed as a critical tool – some would say *the* critical tool – for determining the best oversight of itself.

Considering the professional and commercial incentives for journalists to accurately reflect the public mood in their reporting, the interventionist alignment with moral framing was not unusual. As could be expected based on the economic misery that the crisis had caused, there was abundant evidence that the demonisation of banks, financial services and "Wall Street" resonated with the public in the years after the crisis. In 2012, a poll by Gallup showed Americans' confidence in banking was at its lowest level since the group had begun monitoring this issue annually in 1979 (Jacobe 2012). At the same time, subsequent polling, such as a survey in 2014 by Harris, showed government was even less trusted. Whatever appetite there was for reform in the wake of the crisis became muddied by a wave of anti-statism, itself stirred up by feelings that justice was not being served.

There is always the risk that public polling figures can be cherry-picked to make the case for an argument, a risk that is compounded by differing survey questions, methodologies, terminology and the lack of time-series data for many polls. There are also epistemological critiques of opinion polling data as a means of making knowledge claims. Nonetheless, the results from the Gallup and Harris polling do suggest that the moral framing in the regulatory sample was reflective of a highly negative public mood about the financial industry. While the polling data may not have featured directly in coverage of Dodd-Frank, journalists covering this beat could not help but be aware of such sentiment in the midst of the crisis. Karen Johnson-Cartee notes how journalists rely on public polling, often in problematic ways, as they seek "facts" (Johnson-Cartee 2005, p. 135) to legitimise their accounts.

What remains surprising – in light of the content analysis, the evidence of public attitudes and what is known generally about journalists' behaviour – is that there was not more moral framing, particularly about the sensitive and emotive topic of executive compensation. There was no shortage of opportunities. One example could be seen from a *Washington Post* interview with Chairman Barnie Frank.

In August 2010, a few weeks after the passage of Dodd-Frank, the newspaper interviewed Frank and led on his disclosure that he would hold a hearing on whether regulators were being tough enough in curbing Wall Street pay practices (Goldfarb 2010). The report explained how Dodd-Frank gave regulators powers in terms of how Wall Street firms compensated employees as Frank framed Wall Street executives in terms of their moral weakness and the need for oversight. The article discussed Frank's plans to discuss proposals by the Squam Lake Group. Perplexingly, the *Post* did not cover the hearing itself. Here is a newspaper that has devoted considerable resource to covering the regulation story; it breaks news about plans for a hearing; the hearing concerns a hot topic and will be weeks before mid-term elections, when the country will offer an electoral verdict on the government's crisis performance.

There may be many reasons why the *Post*, and other news services, did not cover the hearing.[2] Dodd-Frank was, by this point, done as a legislative matter; also, the hearing featured experts but no political luminaries apart from Frank. Still, the example suggests the extent to which attention on moral issues, even for a topic as sensitive as Wall Street pay, was limited. Furthermore, the moral framing that did feature in regulatory coverage was generally based on vague references to public anger or superficial descriptions of big business, ordinary people, recklessness by the rich and other tropes. Against a backdrop of indignation. reporters in this sample seemingly were not interested in delving deeply into underlying moral issues. All the while, the chants of Occupy protestors continued to be heard in the capitol.

The view from the newsroom

Assuming the *Post* sample is representative of wider practice, there is a question as to why journalists did not frame discussion more often from a moral perspective. Interviews with reporters at major news services tell a complicated story. Journalists were mindful of the moral dimensions of regulatory reform, and they also had the impression that moral news narratives were dominating the public sphere. Yet they repeatedly indicated a hesitancy to dwell too much on moral issues, in part, it appeared, because of a sense of professionalism. Discussion about moral issues, it seemed, somehow obscured from the "real story," namely the scale and complexity of the job of regulating financial markets. David Enrich spoke of his early days covering the U.S. regulatory story for the *Wall Street Journal*:

> I started viewing the key story as this battle between the forces of good being the Barney Franks of the world, the Sheila Bairs of the world – people like that who were aggressively advocating for a much more hands-on government role, and much tougher laws to curb some of the riskiest activity ... .

> There's a very easy narrative to spin here about (how) the banks, having just survived the biggest crisis since the Great Depression with the help of massive taxpayer bailouts are now pushing or they're fighting against efforts to hold them accountable for anything.

The question of accountability told a richer, more intricate moral tale than the Wall Street/Main Street theme. Paradigmatically, the message of the Wall Street/Main Street dichotomy was simple: The system is unfair system because the rules of the game are different if you are a banker than if you are an ordinary person. The idea supported the interventionist narrative in that it called for the state to level the playing field. But with the accountability theme, moral transgressions compounded each other. *The bankers were paid too much to begin with. Their greed metastasized into recklessness, with devastating results. The bankers awarded themselves large bonuses even after the crisis. The state enabled this behaviour. It bailed out the firms and their shareholders while not prosecuting the bankers.* Each moral wrong was made worse by what followed.

To the extent that journalists did not pursue that story as aggressively as might have been expected, some could have been taking their cues from the Obama administration. Caren Bohan, who reported on the crisis and regulatory reform for Reuters, recalled how reluctant Obama was to engage in the vilification of bankers, even at a time of so much public pain and anger.

> I think he was very mindful of the need to maintain stability in the banking sector, to the point where he was really reluctant to push a populist message about the banks. I remember, I think it was the end of 2009 ... he used the phrase 'fat cats' to describe the bankers,

and there was this big outcry about it.[3] And he never did it again. It goes to the idea that he really believed, and the people around him really believed, that maintaining a sense of calm and stability was more important than shaking things up when it came to the financial sector.

Tom Braithwaite, who covered post-crisis regulatory issues from Washington for the *Financial Times,* said it was apparent in news briefings that there were some in the press corps, such as from the *New York Times*, who were sceptical about the administration's apparent reluctance to prosecute executives involved in the crisis. "Now, I think, consensus is there ought to have been a harsher punishment for some of the executives involved at these institutions. At the time it wasn't immediately a sort of widespread view," Braithwaite said.

In Entman's cascading activation model for considering news framing, the administration has the greatest strength for introducing and promoting frames, which then cascade down to other officials and the media; but the media then are able to transmit – or "activate" – those frames, such that they begin to flow back upwards and influence state actors such as members of Congress. It was a model that Entman used to analyse foreign policy news framing, but it is also useful to consider it with respect to the episode Bohan highlights. Obama's hesitancy to forcefully frame bankers morally set the tone for the wider regulatory narrative in elite media.

There was also a view that focusing on issues such as executive pay detracted from more important issues. David Herszenhorn, who covered Dodd-Frank for the *New York Times*, said: "Every time we talk about capping of bonuses of bankers, everybody's excited because that's something everybody can understand. But when you talk about regulating the multitrillion-dollar derivatives market, people's eyes roll over." For Herszenhorn, the importance of someone being able to buy a Mercedes at the end of the year paled in comparison to the need to regulate synthetic products that threatened the system. "Capping banker bonuses is somehow exciting. It's like, you know, punishing the rich guy," he said, adding that the Gordon Gekko stereotype registered with audiences.

Executive compensation, when discussed in moral terms, offers a binary construction of good and evil. In this case, the villains are bankers, and the victims are ordinary people. Herszenhorn's comments are also borne out by cause frame data from Chapter 3, which showed morally sensitive issues such as pay and reckless behaviour by bankers showing up more than 10 times as often as cause frames involving capital requirements, which regulatory officials had high-lighted as one of the most important issues to address. Although such cause frames may have addressed moral issues, most of these did not double up as moral judgment frames because they were not discussed in explicitly moral terms.

The hesitancy to employ more moral framing also stemmed from the complexity of the issues at hand. Ledyard King of Gannett suggested on one hand that the moral angle was unavoidable. "It was hard not to quote the people who were vilifying the bankers." But on the other, he said deciding who the heroes and villains were was not as straightforward as with a story such as Enron, which had occurred earlier in the decade.

> Maybe the morality of the issue was a little bit more on display (with Enron). It was easier to figure out who the bad guys were. In this case I think it was a little bit more difficult, because, if I recall right, a lot of this was sort of fuelled by real estate speculation, people over-borrowing from lenders who were over-lending ... . So, everyone was kind of in on it.

This idea that everyone was "in on it," as if the crisis came about because of a largescale scam that involved people from all corners, harks back to Narrative 3 in the cause-framing chapter, but it adds a moral twist.

One reporter, who covered the banking industry for a prominent newspaper and asked that her comments be made anonymous, spoke of how good/evil characterisations extended to political debate at the time. She said she resisted the temptation to write in those terms: "It just became so ridiculously, like, you've got to be for one side or the other and the other side is completely evil." She added:

> It's not my job to side with the Republicans or the Democrats. The job is to look at how, practically speaking, to cut through the political jargon and the divisiveness and sort of say this is how this actually would work out.

The reporter said she was proud of how her newspaper avoided taking sides. She, like several other interviewees, saw the act of drawing clear moral distinctions as potentially at odds with accurate reporting: "Our goal is to try to illuminate the truth as much as possible."

Francesco Guerrera, who covered the crisis and Dodd-Frank for the *Financial Times*, said moral issues were difficult for journalists because of personal feelings, particularly if one was covering rich bankers. But he said that reporters are trained to avoid having those thoughts influence coverage.

> As a financial journalist, your job is to get close to these people. Your sources are these people. If you're good, you tend to know a lot about these people and what you see throughout is something that you don't experience in your own life. They are richer, they have lifestyles that you can only dream of. You see them. You may witness things that you consider immoral, for example the lavish expenditure before the crisis … And then you abstract from that and say, 'Well I've got to report what they're doing, whether it's right or wrong, and there are two sides of the coin.'

Guerrera distinguished between financial journalists covering the crisis aftermath and general assignment reporters who had not been exposed to the world of finance and were parachuted in to cover it. He noted that often the latter expressed shock at the lifestyles that banking leaders were leading.

I asked Heather Booth, who directed AFR and as such had an interest in elevating the morality angle, about her impressions of the coverage at the time. She noticed a degree of victim-blaming:

> So, the original story was, I think, perceived as: "Poor people got loans they couldn't repay, and the banks were responsible in giving the poor people those loans, and so the economy fell apart, and maybe the banks were connected with each other and when one fell it was like dominos." I think there were problems with that story in many ways, including the blame placed on the people who were in the communities.

The interviews and content analysis both suggest that most of the moral condemnation was reserved for bankers. At the same time, King's reflective comment and Booth's observation show that there was another media narrative that painted the people who took out large mortgages, in the hopes of getting rich, as morally culpable also. This speaks to an apparently instinctive desire on the part of reporters to classify their subject matter, whether that means treating a tenacious regulator as a hero or treating an overextended homeowner as one of the bad people. Herszenhorn said: "We collectively are guilty of what I call an up-down bias. In search of news, we need winners to become losers, losers to become winners. You know, we need the underdog to rise and the favourite to fall."

A moral vacuum

Here was a case where journalists resisted the attractions of an easy narrative. A moral tale about the crisis and financial regulation was there to be had, but elite news media journalists shied away from telling it. Journalists, in the interviews, indicated they did not want to be moral umpires.

We can see from the *Washington Post* sample that moral framing skewed sharply towards a more interventionist policy paradigm. Yet the relative dearth of moral framing, particularly when compared with frames that focused on economic consequences, may have played a role in shaping wider regulatory discourse. In particular, a policy position that prioritised stability in the banking industry created a significant opportunity for an anti-government movement, one which in turn favoured the market liberal paradigm. Robert Litan of Brookings told me the media narrative surrounding the Obama administration's kid-gloves treatment of bankers – with the bailouts acting as a trigger for the Tea Party – helped fracture American politics.

Obama's crisis response was often compared with that of Franklin Delano Roosevelt in 1933. Such comparisons largely have focused on policy choices, such as when Paul Krugman, in an article for the *New York Times* in November 2008 headlined "Franklin Delano Obama?" (Krugman 2008), stressed the importance of bold spending plans. But a comparison of the moral postures of the two presidents highlights another, arguably starker, difference.

Roosevelt, as noted in Chapter 1, chose not to go down a radical route with his policy towards banks, but he was more than comfortable lambasting bankers in moral terms. Roosevelt's speech to announce his second "New Deal" takes aim at what he called the enemies of peace, including those who engaged in "reckless banking" (Roosevelt 1936). The speech contains one of his most famous remarks as it emphasises a moral distinction between himself and his foes: "They are unanimous in their hate for me – and I welcome their hatred" (Roosevelt 1936). Contrast that with the careful stance that Bohan described Obama as taking and it is clear that the moral messaging from the Obama White House was decidedly more muted. Into that vacuum stepped the Tea Party.

Notes

1 That result was based on a search from 1 June 2009 to 31 March 2012 based on the following terms: "financial crisis" and "regulation" and "(compensation or pay or salaries)."

2 Two Nexis searches – one for the term "Squam Lake" and a separate one for articles that featured both "Barney Frank" and "compensation" – showed only one specialist service, SNL Bank Weekly, covered the hearing.
3 For evidence of the outcry, see Maureen Farrell's story for CNN: "Why Wall Street Hates Obama" (2012). Obama later expressed bemusement that financial figures were upset by criticism that was "extraordinarily mild" (Sorkin 2016).

6   Charting a way forward

In January 2010, a prominent political consultant named Frank Luntz published a 17-page document called *The Language of Financial Reform* (Luntz 2010). It offered opponents of Dodd-Frank a detailed discussion about public attitudes regarding the crisis and tips for how to speak publicly about regulatory proposals. A glimpse of the memo's contents featured in one of the *Washington Post* articles in the sample used for this analysis. The document was also reported on by the *Huffington Post*, which called it a "playbook to help derail financial regulatory reform" (Stein 2010). The *Washington Post* article told of how the memo included a guide of words to use, including "bloated bureaucracy," "big bank bailout bill," "wasteful Washington spending" and "unintended consequences" (Dennis 2010a). The memo acted as a tool for those looking to water down reform and build a narrative to help thwart paradigm shift.

Luntz and his clientele proved effective. In the years that followed the financial crisis, as indicated in the first chapter, the U.S. public's view about the need for regulation appeared to quickly return to its pre-crisis state, one that treated government oversight suspiciously. The success in the 2010 mid-term elections of Tea Party candidates, with their calls for less government, offered one sign of this. Public polling trends offered another.

Attempts to redefine the terms of discourse are the stock and trade of the PR industry. The journalist David Enrich in Chapter 3 spoke of an "army" of people ready to engage with the press to get their messages across. He separately talked of interest groups that were flush with money, eager to offer the telling anecdote that could make their case. Enrich's language conjures up war room scenarios where the powerful marshal the forces at their disposal to win the message battle of the day. Such images may sound like Hollywood fare, but a March 2021 article in the *New Yorker* suggests they may not be far from

DOI: 10.4324/9781003177944-6

reality. Jane Mayer (2021) wrote of a private conference call featuring a policy advisor for Republican Senator Mitch McConnell and Kyle McKenzie, the research director for a group run by billionaire Charles Koch's network. In the call, McKenzie spoke of the vast resources that had been poured into finding a message to thwart a popular voting reform effort (Mayer 2021).

The memo that Luntz wrote was published by a public relations firm he ran called The Word Doctors. The firm's LinkedIn page has noted that he has had a track record in reframing ideologically charged terms:

> In the political arena, our CEO, Dr. Frank Luntz, is known for helping change the public vocabulary – he transformed the "estate tax" into the "the death tax," moved the public debate from "school vouchers" to "opportunity scholarships," and re-cast "drilling for oil" as "exploring for energy." (The Word Doctors n.d.)

The LinkedIn page indicates a readiness on Luntz's part to openly advertise the nature of his trade. That is in stark contrast with the clandestine work by the Koch-backed group. In the 2010 case, Luntz's transparency about such "efforts to change the public vocabulary" became newsworthy, as seen by the attention devoted to the memo by the *Huffington Post* and the *Washington Post*. In chronicling these efforts, the reporters were demonstrating they were not taken in by spin. Indeed, the journalists I interviewed showed a keen awareness of the degree to which news sources sought to frame regulatory issues.

Still, despite such awareness, and evidence that many reporters worked hard to avoid being spun when covering Dodd-Frank, it is also clear that Luntz's ideas, if not his exact terminology, repeatedly found a home at two of the country's leading newspapers. Some of this was inevitable; when key actors make important public statements, journalists often have little choice but to report them. If those actors are effective at framing issues a certain way, that will appear in the news coverage. But the focus of this book has been to trace the frequency of certain ideas. In that sense, it is clear that there was a readiness within elite media to feature news framing that was aligned with a market liberal paradigm, particularly when predictive claims were being made.

The results of this analysis are not meant to suggest that these newspapers somehow drilled into people's minds the idea that market liberalism was the way forward, like some modern-day version of the discredited hypodermic needle theory. Rather, they are meant to show the ways that the journalism industry – wittingly or otherwise – can remained attached to a set of ideas despite developments that point in a different direction. If the financial crisis represents an anomaly that highlighted a major deficiency in the market liberal paradigm, why would journalists continue to feature so much framing that aligned with that paradigm? It is true that in writing about crisis causes, the samples showed more interventionist framing. Yet in writing about regulatory consequences, it was the opposite. Meanwhile, framing that focused on the moral dimensions of the regulatory story was largely absent.

The economist John Quiggan, writing not long after the financial crisis erupted, used the term "zombie economics" to highlight policy ideas that he argued had been shown to be wrong but still refused to die (Quiggan 2010). Paul Krugman has also taken up this theme (Krugman 2020). These economists have focused on showing logical fallacies and damning evidence with regard to specific policies. The work I have presented is less concerned with policies per se as it is with how certain ways of thinking can seep into a national discourse. It is a subtle process, observable by focusing on the repetition of news frames. The leap I am making – and it is a leap – is that the work of researchers like Luntz, and more recently McKenzie, is linked to the repetition of certain ideas in the press.

Pattern detection

In a hypermediated world, the phrase "media narrative" has become commonplace, tossed about freely by media figures, scholars and political actors. But providing systematic evidence about such narratives is a complicated exercise. It requires a means by which one can observe and categorise the components of the narratives. The methodology developed here allows for such analysis. The media narrative is situated within a conceptual framework, where it supports paradigms and ideologies, and it is supported by news frames.

What the analysis has shown is that actors who favoured a market liberal paradigm – mostly political actors but also independent elites and financial industry figures – focused on the frames that they had reason to believe resonated with the public. Where the battle was likely to be unsuccessful, such as with crisis causes or moral issues, they ceded ground. But even there they made the most of the situation to shore up the pre-crisis paradigm. In the case of crisis causes, financial industry figures appeared to make a strategic decision to stay out of the press while maintaining relationships with sympathetic state actors and arguing in Congressional committees that no one could have seen the crisis coming. Meanwhile, independent elites and political actors used the Congressional inquiry as a platform to push a theory that government policies caused the financial crisis, finding some modest success within news media despite clear scepticism from experienced journalists.

In the case of consequence frames, those aiming to thwart paradigm shift accomplished two remarkable feats. They were able to suggest that Dodd-Frank's efforts to reduce systemic risk and tackle the too-big-to-fail issue would lead to more bailouts rather than less; and they managed to achieve an overwhelming advantage in the frequency of market liberal frames that decried regulation as an unfair, bureaucratic, job-killing infringement on the economy. Finally, with moral frames, journalists showed less interest in pursuing that story, a tendency that enabled pro-market actors to flip the script and suggest the reform-minded Obama administration was not interested in moral justice.

The first chapter highlighted a concern with news media's pre-crisis posture and the possibility they had acted as cheerleaders for the financial sector rather than as a watchdog for society. If that concern was valid, there is even greater reason to be focused on news media behaviour after the crisis. The case studies for each of the chapters in this book do not show a uniform picture. The divergence in framing patterns suggests journalists behaved differently depending on the nature of the subject at hand. But a common theme in each case was a readiness to distrust government. This is normally a starting point for the watchdog role, but not necessarily if the press is also meant to be a watchdog for private-sector abuses. The data point to a news media industry that had not fully abandoned its market-cheerleader posture and/or one where journalists were more susceptible to actors' agenda-building efforts than they might have realised. Further study with larger samples would be needed to confirm these initial findings, to better understand such divergent patterns and to rule out the possibility of statistical flukes.

Paradigmatic shifts, as noted earlier, can take place over many years. This was the case with the shift to Keynesian interventionism and, even more so, with the initial embrace of a market liberal paradigm in the 1970s. In that respect, it is still too soon to say that the dominance of market liberalism, as we have known it, was not eroded by the financial crisis. The election in 2016 of Donald Trump in the United States, with his campaign promises to "gut" Dodd-Frank, seemed to suggest that market liberalism was back on the march. Yet, Dodd-Frank was not gutted as many of the interventionist measures in the law survived (Taylor 2018). Furthermore, the COVID-19 pandemic set in motion large-scale government economic intervention that far eclipsed what took place in 2008 and 2009.

To be sure, the economic policy response to the pandemic has been an unorthodox affair. The amount of suffering has been far greater than that experienced in 2008, which itself was on a scale not seen for decades. As such, decisions to spend trillions of dollars on economic support for people and companies should be seen as akin to crisis management following a natural disaster rather than a coherent, ideologically driven set of policies. Nonetheless, there is now, arguably, the possibility that new narratives develop around the idea that government can be a solution, not a problem, in direct opposition to Reagan's famous message.

The quantitative framing approach taken here holds the promise of identifying undetected patterns within journalism. This methodology enables us to see the divergence in patterns between the backward-looking cause frames and forward-looking consequence frames, a divergence that is not initially obvious. The findings raise pointed questions about the capacity of journalists to challenge entrenched views about the state and the supposed self-corrective properties of the markets. Where else might such analysis reveal hitherto unseen tendencies in coverage? News coverage of three areas, each of which has become increasingly prominent in the past decade, stand out: climate change, the effects of "big tech" on society and public health.

All three areas share an important feature with financial regulation in that they are complex subjects; writing about them requires deep knowledge if one is to go beyond surface claims. Indeed, if one subscribes to the analysis of economists such as Quiggan and Krugman, the survival of "zombie ideas" requires either a readiness to accept surface claims or to disregard evidence. In all three cases, the role of the state versus that of the market is central to the way these subjects are characterised.

Returning to watchdog journalism, the governing idea behind such a role is the notion of public accountability. When Dean Starkman wrote that the watchdog did not bite (2014), he highlighted ways in which accountability for financial sector behaviour was lacking. But accountability requires a shared sense of probity, and the paradigms of the day should, in theory, help provide that. Paradigms govern public perceptions about the way in which technological companies are able to make use of algorithms in the marketplace, the way that public health is provided and paid for, and the ways that renewable energy is incentivised, or harmful emissions are dealt with. To the extent that news framing leans towards one paradigm or another can, I would argue, make the difference in what narratives emerge in these vital areas.

This leads to another, more urgent question: What should journalists do? If they are vulnerable to sophisticated agenda-building techniques by actors with vested interests, how can they report on the burning issues of the day without becoming tools in paradigmatic contests? Or, should they clearly engage in such contestation?

A more robust journalism

An old model for journalistic behaviour held that there should be a balanced, two-sides approach to any issue that was not settled. Jay Rosen (2009), in "He said, she said journalism: Lame formula in the land of the active user," argued this kneejerk response left the journalist in the centre of two polarised extremes. I would add that from a paradigmatic perspective, such a result will often be a victory for the status quo. This is the same critique of climate coverage that dutifully includes "the other side" regardless of the strength of evidence on one side of the ledger. But if an automatic tendency towards both-sides-ism is problematic, would society be better served by crusading, one-sided coverage? Matthew Levendusky (2013) suggests this is what now routinely occurs in an era of partisan media, leading more citizens to distrust each other and become uncompromising.

Nikki Usher has argued that business journalism needs a more active watchdog role. She wrote: "Thus, this approach means reconceiving watchdog journalism as a kind of storytelling that is intended to provide direction and clear guidance for action" (Usher 2013, p. 14). This reimagining of the role, she argued, could force journalists to be more accountable when the storytelling was ineffective. Usher here is connecting watchdog journalism with the power of narrative. A challenge will be whether journalists can achieve the effective storytelling Usher describes but avoid doing so purely to serve partisan objectives.

None of the journalists I interviewed worked for an organisation whose news desk operated on partisan lines. All of them displayed a commitment to some form of "truth-squadding." They also shared a sense of responsibility to operate independently and to avoid being swayed by actors who had ideological agendas. But the content analysis would suggest that the industry's collective ability to achieve these aims is very much a work in progress.

Elite media, due to their inter-media agenda-setting properties, have a particular responsibility to recognise the ways ideas can infiltrate news coverage and create narratives. But at a time when well-financed actors invest vast resources to identify and deploy winning messages, what might constitute an effective journalistic response? The research here points to three priorities for countering the agenda-building aims of powerful interests: (1) a greater awareness of how framing helps to establish and reinforce narratives; (2) increased attention on the special properties of predictive appeals; and (3) a recognition of the role of storytelling as part of the watchdog role. Regarding the first of these priorities, Robert Entman proposed considering framing within a broader conceptual framework to understand bias. Writing just before the financial crisis struck, he suggested that persistent patterns of content bias mean news media "may be systematically assisting certain entities to induce their preferred behaviour in others" (Entman 2007, p. 166). Bias can occur at so many points in the news production and news consumption processes (Hamborg, Donnay and Gipp 2019). This is what agenda-building actors seek to take advantage of. By extending Entman's idea about content patterns to the ideological dimension of news framing within running stories, we may gain a greater understanding of modern agenda-building techniques.

But when discussing journalistic practice, we also need to be realistic. Framing at a sentence-by-sentence level is rarely likely to be the result of deliberation. The speed at which journalists are expected to work and the competing professional demands they face prohibit that level of introspection. Earlier it was suggested that the choices in framing will often be the result of unconscious biases or the tactics of skilful agenda-builders (or a combination of both). It's worth adding that not all of these biases will be ideological in nature; some will come from professional incentives. But that makes journalists even more vulnerable.

For instance, journalists have strong professional incentives to get and use powerful quotes for their articles. They know that such quotes lead to more praise from editors, more readers and more career success. But that can be exploited by those looking to establish their chosen narratives. In the *Washington Post* sample, 32% of frames from direct quotes had a market liberal orientation. That was noticeably higher than the 19% share of market liberal frames in the overall sample. My reading of this data is that those reinforcing the market liberal paradigm were simply more adept at media manipulation. They understood journalists are always on the lookout for strong soundbites and they took advantage of that.

It would be foolish to suggest that journalists, when going through their notes, should pause to think about the framing they are employing. If my own experience of newsroom culture is anything to go by, that will never happen. But there can be a greater understanding of the amount of effort actors put into getting their viewpoints across. When these actors offer vivid quotes and captivating anecdotes, journalists can at least be aware of the goods that are being sold to them.

Regarding the second priority, Jennifer Jerit has argued that the study of predictive appeals within communication deserves greater attention. Jerit, James Kuklinski and Paul Quirk (2009) offer two case studies, one from the mid-19th century and another from the late 20th century, in which politicians made arguments largely from discussion about imagined futures. The case studies illustrate how politicians make predictions to provoke fear, anger and other strong feelings. "They also show that neither politicians nor the media seem to provide citizens with reliable, readily identified cues to help distinguish those that are worth taking seriously from those that are just hot air" (Jerit, Kuklinski and Quirk 2009, p. 114).

There is a "'twas-ever-thus" element to this issue, as indicated by the nearly 150-year span of the cases studies those authors chose. But as communications technology has grown faster and more sophisticated, the mismatch between ultrafast messaging and slow policy feedback mechanisms has only grown wider. Put simply, audiences are subject to more predictive messages in more targeted ways, while their ability to evaluate the validity of those messages has not got much better. Meanwhile, as media organisations are subject to the loss of institutional memory, a form of media amnesia takes hold, one facilitated by the atomisation of news that the journalist Simon Denyer described in Chapter 4.[1] Journalistically, this calls for greater emphasis on an old tradition: scepticism. There are tentative signs of a more sceptical press in the wake of the crisis. Lauren Furey, Moonhee Cho and Tiffany Mohr (2019) compared coverage of corporate social responsibility before and after the crisis. They found evidence that journalists were not as quick to adopt the company line as in the past.

The third priority has been highlighted in work by scholars such as Usher and Mark McBeth, Robert Tokle and Susan Schaefer (2018). Journalists, if they want their reporting to register, will need to go further in acknowledging the intrinsic power that narratives have in a media-saturated world. An example of this power comes from one of the articles in the Dodd-Frank sample. In the penultimate paragraph of the article that reported on the Luntz memo, *Washington Post* journalist Brady Dennis described an intense effort to neuter the legislation:

> ... the financial industry has poured months of effort and millions of dollars into advertisements, political contributions and lobbying efforts, with the goal of shaping the legislation and killing elements they say would stifle innovation and increase the cost of business. (Dennis 2010a)

The reporter here is adding an important storyline to the coverage, namely who was paying for what messaging. The phrase "follow the money" (itself invented for narrative purposes[2]) may be a cliché but that does not make it less relevant. This storyline, in fact, rarely came up in the Dodd-Frank coverage. For those who believe that the actors with the largest war chests should not automatically be the victors in public debate, this was a missed opportunity to build a better narrative of their own. Either way, journalists will need to recognise that effective watchdog journalism will increasingly require effective narratives.

When considering the interviews I conducted, I am left with the strong impression that many reporters and editors do recognise the importance of the priorities suggested here. But other actors, seeking to influence the behaviour of the press, have their own priorities. These actors not only have enormous resources but also new tools in an algorithm-dominated media landscape. As new battles to establish narratives are waged, journalists will have their work cut out for them.

Notes

1 Laura Basu's *Media Amnesia* (2018) explores many of the same themes as I have here, but looking at British media coverage of the crisis aftermath.
2 The phrase came from the screenwriter William Goldman in the script for the movie *All the President's Men* (Goldman 2000).

References

111th Congress. (2010). *Dodd-Frank Wall Street Reform and Consumer Protection Act*. Washington, DC: U.S. Government Printing Office.

Acharya, V., Cooley, T., Richardson, M. and Walter, I. (2010). *Regulating Wall Street: The Dodd-Frank Act and the New Architecture of Global Finance*. Hoboken, NJ: John Wiley & Sons.

Aikins, S.K. (2009). 'Political Economy of Government Intervention in the Free Market System'. *Administrative Theory & Praxis*, 31(3), 403–408.

Aldrich, J.H., Bishop, B.H., Hatch, R.S., Hillygus, D.S. and Rhode, D.W. (2013). 'Blame, Responsibility, and the Tea Party in the 2010 Midterm Elections'. *Political Behavior*, 36(3), 471–491.

Americans for Financial Reform. (2009). *AFR: "Too Big to Fail" Legislation Needs to Be Improved to Ensure We Avoid Another Financial Meltdown* [press release]. 30 October.

Andrews, E. (2008). 'Greenspan Concedes Error on Regulation'. *New York Times*, 23 October.

Andrews, E. (2009). 'Bernanke, a Hero to His Own, Can't Shake Critics in Congress'. *The New York Times*, 20 August.

Appelbaum, B. (2009a). 'Obama Defends Financial Overhaul; Fault Lines Emerge as Industry Groups Blast Plan to Create Consumer Agency'. *The Washington Post*, 18 June.

Appelbaum, B. (2009b). 'Obama Administration Pushing for Regulatory Reform on Many Fronts'. *The New York Times*, 23 September.

Bach, T., Weber, M. and Quiring, O. (2013). 'News frames, inter-media frame transfer and the financial crisis'. *Zeszyty Prasoznawcze*, 56(1), 90–110.

Baily, M.N. (2010). 'Executive Compensation Oversight after the Dodd-Frank Wall Street Reform and Consumer Protection Act'. Brookings Institution.

Baily, M.N. and Elliott, D.J. (2009). 'Telling the Narrative of the Financial Crisis: Not Just a Housing Bubble'. Brookings Institution.

Baker, P. (2011). 'Obama's Jobs Search'. *The New York Times*, 23 January.

Baker, D. and McArthur, T. (2009). 'The Value of the "Too Big to Fail" Big Bank Subsidy'. Center for Economic and Policy Research.

Barr, M. (2011). 'Ending Too Big to Fail'. Brookings Institution.

Barth, J.R., Brumbaugh, R.D. and Wilcox, J.A. (2000). 'The Repeal of Glass-Steagall and the Advent of Broad Banking'. *Journal of Economic Perspectives*, 14(2), 191–204.

Barthes, R. (1957). *Mythologies*. Paris: Éditions du Seuil.

Basu, L. (2018). *Media Amnesia: Rewriting the Economic Crisis*. London: Pluto Press.

Berkowitz, D. (1992). 'Who Sets the Media Agenda? The Ability of Policymakers to Determine News Decisions', in Kennamer, J.D., ed. *Public Opinion, the Press, and Public Policy*. Westport, CT: Praeger.

Berry, M. (2012). 'The *Today* Programme and the Banking Crisis'. *Journalism*, 14(2), 253–270.

Bishin, B.G. (2003). 'Independently Validating Ideology Measures: A Look at NOMINATE and Adjusted ADA Scores'. *American Politics Research*, 31(4), 401–425.

Bishop, G.F. (2004). *The Illusion of Public Opinion: Fact and Artifact in American Public Opinion Polls*. Lanham, MD: Rowman & Littlefield Publishers.

Bjerke, P. and Fonn, B.K. (2015). 'A Hidden Theory in Financial Crisis Journalism? The Case of Norway'. *Nordicom Review*, 36(2), 113–127.

Blinder, A.S. (2008). 'Keynesian Economics', in Henderson, D.R., ed. *Concise Encyclopedia of Economics*. Indianapolis, IN: The Library of Economics and Liberty.

Block, F. (2008). 'Polanyi's Double Movement and the Reconstruction of Critical Theory'. *Revue Interventions économiques*, 38, 20–36.

Bordo, M.D. (2008). 'An Historical Perspective on the Crisis of 2007–2008'. NBER Working Paper No. 14569, National Bureau of Economic Research.

Borio, C. and White, W.R. (2003). 'Whither Monetary and Financial Stability: The Implications of Evolving Policy Regimes'. Bank for International Settlements Working Paper No. 147, Bank for International Settlements.

Boykoff, J. and Laschever, E. (2011). 'The Tea Party Movement, Framing, and the US Media'. *Social Movement Studies*, 10(4), 341–366.

Brüggemann, M. (2014). 'Between Frame Setting and Frame Sending: How Journalists Contribute to News Frames'. *Communication Theory*, 24(1), 61–82.

Buchanan, J.M. (1978). 'Markets, States, and the Extent of Morals'. *The American Economic Review*, 68, 364–368.

Butler, E. (n.d.). *A Short History of the Mont Pèlerin Society*. The Mont Pèlerin Society. Available at: https://www.montpelerin.org/about-mps/

Butterick, K.J. (2015). *Collusion and Complacency: A Critical Introduction to Business and Financial Journalism*. London: Pluto Press.

Calmes, J. (2010a). 'With Populist Stance, Obama Takes on Banks'. *The New York Times*, 22 January.

Calmes, J. (2010b). 'A Testy Exchange Over Jobs Proposals'. *The New York Times*, 10 December.

Calmes, J. and Chan. S. (2010). 'Obama Chooses Warren to Set Up Consumer Bureau'. *The New York Times*, 18 September.

Campbell, A.L. (2010). 'The Public's Role in Winner-Take-All Politics'. *Politics & Society*, 38(2), 227–232.

Canova, T.A. (2009). 'Financial Market Failure as a Crisis in the Rule of Law: From Market Fundamentalism to a New Keynesian Regulatory Model'. *Harvard Law & Policy Review*, 3(2), 369–396.

Capra, F. (1939). *Mr. Smith Goes to Washington* [Motion picture]. United States: Columbia Pictures.

Capra, F. (1946). *It's A Wonderful Life* [Motion picture]. United States: RKO Radio Pictures.

Cawley, A. (2012). 'Sharing the Pain or Shouldering the Burden? News-media Framing of the Public Sector and the Private Sector in Ireland during the Economic Crisis, 2008–2010'. *Journalism Studies*, 13(4), 600–615.

Chakravartty, P. and Schiller, D. (2010). 'Global Financial Crisis| Neoliberal Newspeak and Digital Capitalism in Crisis'. *International Journal of Communication*, 4, 670–692.

Chan, S. (2010). 'Dodd Denounces Pace of Banking Overhaul'. *The New York Times*, 5 February.

Chang, H.-J. (1997). 'The Economics and Politics of Regulation'. *Cambridge Journal of Economics*, 21(6), 703–728.

Cho, D. (2009). 'Banks 'Too Big to Fail' Have Grown Even Bigger'. *The Washington Post*, 28 August.

Cho, D. (2010). 'Wall St. Loophole Remains in Bill; Investment Firms Can Bypass Some Rules in Running Banks'. *The Washington Post*, 19 May.

Cho, D. and Appelbaum, B. (2009). 'Bank Repayments May Exceed Estimate; Firms That Passed Government Stress Tests to Be Cleared to Return Federal Aid'. *The Washington Post*, 6 June.

Cho, D. and Dennis, B. (2010a). 'Obama May Bend on Consumer Agency; White House Open to Compromise to Pass Financial Regulation'. *The Washington Post*, 25 February.

Cho, D. and Dennis, B. (2010b). 'Senate Panel Passes Financial Regulation Bill; Consumer Agency in Fed; Obama's Agenda Takes Another Big Step'. *The Washington Post*, 23 March.

Cho, D., Goldfarb, Z.A. and Tse, M.T. (2009). 'U.S. Targets Excessive Pay for Top Executives; Compensation Czar to Oversee Firms at Heart of Crisis'. *The Washington Post*, 11 June.

Chomsky, N. (1997). 'What Makes Mainstream Media Mainstream'. *Z Magazine*.

CNBC (2010). 'US Does Not Have Capitalism Now: Stiglitz'. CNBC.com.

CNN/Opinion Research Corporation (2009). Poll: TARP not working; don't spend more, Americans say. CNN. Available at: https://politicalticker.blogs.cnn.com/2009/01/16/poll-tarp-not-working-dont-spend-more-americans-say/

Coffee, J.C.J. (2013). 'Extraterritorial Financial Regulation: Why E.T. Can't Come Home'. *Cornell Law Review*, 99(6), 1259–1297.

Cohen, B.C. (1963). *The Press and Foreign Policy*. Princeton, NJ: Princeton University Press.

Cohen, S. (1973). *Folk Devils and Moral Panics: The Creation of the Mods and Rockers*. London: Paladin.

Core, J.E. and Guay, W.R. (2010). 'Is There a Case for Regulating Executive Pay in the Financial Services Industry?'. Working Paper, Wharton School, University of Pennsylvania.

Corner, J. (2003). 'Debate: The Model in Question – A Response to Klaehn on Herman and Chomsky'. *European Journal of Communication*, 18(3), 367–375.

Covert, T.J.A. and Wasburn, P.C. (2007). 'Measuring Media Bias: A Content Analysis of *Time* and *Newsweek* Coverage of Domestic Social Issues 1975–2000'. *Social Science Quarterly*, 88(3), 690–706.

Crawford, C. (2011). 'The Repeal of the Glass-Steagall Act and the Current Financial Crisis'. *Journal of Business and Economic Research*, 9(1), 128–130.

Crotty, J. (2011). 'The Realism of Assumptions Does Matter: Why Keynes-Minsky Theory Must Replace Efficient Market Theory as the Guide to Financial Regulation Policy'. Working Paper No. 2011–05, UMass Amherst Economics.

Crouch, C. (2009). 'Privatised Keynesianism: An Unacknowledged Policy Regime'. *The British Journal of Politics and International Relations*, 11(3), 382–399.

Cunningham, B. (2003). 'Re-thinking Objectivity'. *Columbia Journalism Review*, 42(2), 24–32.

Curran, J. (2002). *Media and Power*. London: Routledge.

Damstra, A. and Vliegenthart, R. (2018). '(Un) covering the Economic Crisis? Over-time and Inter-media Differences in Salience and Framing'. *Journalism Studies*, 19(7), 983–1003.

Day, K. (1999a). 'Banking Accord Likely to Be Law; Clinton Hails Hard-Reached Agreement'. *The Washington Post*, 23 October.

Day, K. (1999b). 'Reinventing the Bank; With Depression-Era Law About to Be Rewritten, the Future Remains Unclear'. *The Washington Post*, 31 October.

Dennis, B. (2010a). 'Campaign Builds for Consumer Protection Agency; Advocates Counter Banks' Push Against Stand-alone Unit'. *The Washington Post*, 11 February.

Dennis, B. (2010b). 'New Regulation Bill, Same Outlook; No GOP Support for New Plan; Dodd's Concessions Yield Few Gains in Senate'. *The Washington Post*, 16 March.

Dennis, B. (2010c). 'Senate Votes for More Fed Oversight; Compromise Passes 96 to 0; Measure to Cut Loose Fannie, Freddie Fails'. *The Washington Post*, 12 May.

Dennis, B. (2010d). 'Battle Looms over New Financial Watchdog; Liberals Back Harvard Law Professor for Top Job, but Others Are Wary'. *The Washington Post*, 20 July.

Dennis, B. and Kane, P. (2010). 'Senators Near Deal on Financial Overhaul; Bipartisan Consensus Could Allow Debate to Begin Next Week'. *The Washington Post*, 22 April.

Dennis, B. and Murray, S. (2010). 'Regulatory Bill Gets Bipartisan Push; Senate Passes Amendments; Measure to Cut Risk in Bailouts Wins 93 Votes'. *The Washington Post*, 6 May.

de Vreese, C.H., Peter, J. and Semetko, H.A. (2001). 'Framing Politics at the Launch of the Euro: A Cross-national Comparative Study of Frames in the News'. *Political Communication*, 18(2), 107–122.

Dodd, C., (2010). 'Implementing the Dodd-Frank Wall Street Reform and Consumer Protection Act, Transcript'. U.S. Government Printing Office, 30 September.

Dogan, M. (1996). 'The Hybridization of Social Science Knowledge – Navigating Among the Disciplines: The Library and Interdisciplinary Inquiry'. *Library Trends*, 45(2), 296–314.

Dymski, G.A. (2011). 'The Global Crisis and the Governance of Power in Finance', in Arestis, P., Sobreira, R. and Oreiro, J.L., eds. *The Financial Crisis: Origins and Implications*. London: Palgrave Macmillan.

Elder, C.D. and Cobb, R.W. (1984). 'Agenda-Building and the Politics of Aging'. *Policy Studies Journal*, 13, 115–129.

Elliott, D.J. (2012). 'The Volcker Rule and Its Impact on the U.S. Economy'. Brookings Institution.

Entman, R.M. (1993). 'Framing: Toward Clarification of a Fractured Paradigm'. *Journal of Communication*, 43(4), 51–58.

Entman, R.M. (2003). 'Cascading Activation: Contesting the White House's Frame After 9/11'. *Political Communication*, 20(4), 415–432.

Entman, R.M. (2007). 'Framing Bias: Media in the Distribution of Power. *Journal of Communication*, 57(1), 163–173.

Entman, R.M. and Usher, N. (2018). 'Framing in a Fractured Democracy: Impacts of Digital Technology on Ideology, Power and Cascading Network Activation'. *Journal of Communication*, 68(2), 298–308.

Falasca, K. (2014). 'Framing the Financial Crisis: An Unexpected Interaction Between the Government and the Press'. *Observatorio*, 8(1), 1–21.

Farnsworth, S.J. and Lichter, S.R. (2005). 'The Mediated Congress: Coverage of Capitol Hill in the *New York Times* and the *Washington Post*'. *Harvard International Journal of Press/Politics*, 10(2), 94–107.

Farrell, M. (2012). 'Why Wall Street Hates Obama'. CNNMoney, 6 November.

Financial Crisis Inquiry Commission. (2011). *The Financial Crisis Inquiry Report: Final Report of the National Commission on the Causes of the Financial and Economic Crisis in the United States* 2011. Washington, DC.

Fitzgerald, F.S. (1925). *The Great Gatsby*. New York, NY: Charles Scribner's Sons.

Fletcher, M.A. (2011). 'Is There a GOP Housing Remedy?'. *The Washington Post*, 31 December.

Fraser, M. (2009). 'Five Reasons for Crash Blindness'. *British Journalism Review*, 20, 78–83.

Free to Choose. (1980). Public Broadcasting Service.

Free to Choose Network. (2012). https://www.youtube.com/watch?v= 14gM0HK7sQU (accessed 15 December 2021).

Freeden, M. (2003). *Ideology: A Very Short Introduction*. Oxford: Oxford University Press.

Furey, L.D., Cho, M. and Mohr, T.L. (2019). 'Is Business News Starting to Bark? How Business News Covers Corporate Social Responsibility Post the Economic Crisis'. *Journalism*, 20(2), 256–273.

Gallup (2020). 'Big Business'. Gallup. Available at: https://news.gallup.com/poll/5248/big-business.aspx

Galtung, J. and Ruge, M.H. (1965). 'The Structure of Foreign News: The Presentation of the Congo, Cuba and Cyprus Crises in Four Norwegian Newspapers'. *Journal of Peace Research*, 2(1), 64–90.

Gamson, W.A. and Modigliani, A. (1987). 'The Changing Culture of Affirmative Action', in Braungart, R.D., ed. *Research in Political Sociology*, Vol. 3. Greenwich, CT: JAI Press.

Gamson, W.A. and Modigliani, A. (1989) 'Media Discourse and Public Opinion on Nuclear Power: A Constructionist Approach'. *American Journal of Sociology*, 95(1), 1–37.

Glinavos, I. (2010). 'Regulation and the Role of Law in Economic Crisis'. *European Business Law Review*, 21(4), 539–558.

Goffman, E. (1974). *Frame Analysis: An Essay of the Organization of Experience*. New York, NY: Harper and Row.

Golan, G. (2006). 'Inter-Media Agenda Setting and Global News Coverage'. *Journalism Studies*, 7(2), 323–333.

Goldfarb, Z.A. (2010). 'Frank Plans Hearing on Wall St. Pay'. *The Washington Post*, 25 August.

Goldman, W. (2000). *Five Screenplays with Essays*. New York and London: Applause.

Grant, J.K. (2010). 'What the Financial Services Industry Puts Together Let No Person Put Asunder: How the Gramm-Leach-Bliley Act Contributed to the 2008–2009 American Capital Markets Crisis'. *Albany Law Review*, 73(2), 371–419.

Greenspan, A. (1999). *Insurance Companies and Banks under the New Regulatory Law. Remarks before a meeting of the American Council of Life Insurance*. The Federal Reserve Board, 15 November.

Gregg, P., Jewell, S. and Tonks, I. (2012). 'Executive Pay and Performance: Did Bankers' Bonuses Cause the Crisis?'. *International Review of Finance*, 12(1), 89–122.

Groseclose, T. and Milyo, J. (2005). 'A Measure of Media Bias'. *Quarterly Journal of Economics*, 120(4), 1191–1237.

Guardino, M. and Snyder, D. (2012). 'The Tea Party and the Crisis of Neoliberalism: Mainstreaming New Right Populism in the Corporate News Media'. *New Political Science*, 34(4), 527–548.

Guerrera, F. (2009). 'Why Generalists Were Not Equipped to Cover the Complexities of the Crisis'. *Ethical Space – International Journal of Communication Ethics*, 6(Special Issue), 43–49.

Habermas, J. (1991). *The Structural Transformation of the Public Sphere: An Inquiry into a Category of Bourgeois Society*. Cambridge, MA: MIT Press.

Hall, P.A. (1993). 'Policy Paradigms, Social Learning, and the State: The Case of Economic Policymaking in Britain'. *Comparative Politics*, 25(3), 275–296.

Hall, S. (1973). 'Encoding and Decoding in the Television Discourse', in During, S., ed. *The Cultural Studies Reader*. New York, NY: Routledge, 90–103.

Hamborg, F., Donnay, K. and Gipp, B. (2019). 'Automated Identification of Media Bias in News Articles: An Interdisciplinary Literature Review'. *International Journal on Digital Libraries*, 20(4), 391–415.

Harcup, T. and O'Neill, D. (2001). 'What Is News? Galtung and Ruge Revisited'. *Journalism Studies*, 2(2), 261–280.

Hayek, F.A. (1944). *The Road to Serfdom*. Chicago, IL: University of Chicago Press.

Helleiner, E. (1996). *States and the Reemergence of Global Finance: From Bretton Woods to the 1990s*. Ithaca, NY: Cornell University Press.

Hendrickson, J.M. (2001). 'The Long and Bumpy Road to Glass-Steagall Reform: A Historical and Evolutionary Analysis of Banking Legislation'. *The American Journal of Economics and Sociology*, 60(4), 849–879.

Herman, E.S. and Chomsky, N. (1988). *Manufacturing Consent: The Political Economy of the Mass Media*. New York, NY: Pantheon.

Herszenhorn, D.M. (2010). 'Finance Overhaul Approved by House'. *The New York Times*, 1 July.

Herszenhorn, D.M. and Wyatt, E. (2010). 'Banking Bill Negotiations Begin Again'. *The New York Times*, 21 April.

Jacobe, D. (2008). 'Six in 10 Oppose Wall Street Bailouts'. Gallup. Available at: https://news.gallup.com/poll/106114/six-oppose-wall-street-bailouts.aspx

Jacobe, D. (2012). 'Job Growth Demands Restoring Confidence in Banks'. Gallup. Available at: https://news.gallup.com/businessjournal/158414/job-growth-demands-restoring-confidence-banks.aspx

Jerit, J. (2009). 'How Predictive Appeals Affect Policy Opinions'. *American Journal of Political Science*, 53(2), 411–426.

Jerit, J., Kuklinski, J.H. and Quirk, P.J. (2009). 'Strategic Politicians, Emotional Citizens, and the Rhetoric of Prediction', in Borgida, E., Federico, C.M., Sullivan, J.L., eds. *The Political Psychology of Democratic Citizenship*. Oxford: Oxford University Press.

John, D. (1999). 'Gramm-Leach-Bliley Act (S. 900): A Major Step Toward Financial Deregulation'. The Heritage Foundation.

Johnson-Cartee, K.S. (2005). *News Narratives and News Framing: Constructing Political Reality*. Lanham, MD: Rowman & Littlefield Publishers.

Jones, M.D. and McBeth, M.K. (2010). 'A Narrative Policy Framework: Clear Enough to be Wrong?'. *Policy Studies Journal*, 38(2), 329–353.

Jones, J. (2013). 'Record High in U.S. say Big Government Greatest Threat'. Gallup. Available at: https://news.gallup.com/poll/166535/record-high-say-big-government-greatest-threat.aspx

Keynes, J.M. (1936). *The General Theory of Employment, Interest and Money*. London: Macmillan.

Kling, A. (2010). 'Policy Report: The Era of Expert Failure'. Cato Institute.

Knowles, S., Phillips, G. and Lidberg, J.K.E. (2017). 'Reporting the Global Financial Crisis'. *Journalism Studies*, 18(3), 322–340.

Krugman, P. (2008). 'Franklin Delano Obama?'. *The New York Times*, 10 November.

Krugman, P. (2020). *Arguing with Zombies: Economics, Politics, and the Fight for a Better Future*. New York, NY: W.W. Norton and Company.

Kuhn, T.S. (1970). *The Structure of Scientific Revolutions*, 2nd Edition. Chicago, IL: University of Chicago Press.

Kuttner, R. (1999). 'De-Re-Regulation'. *The Washington Post*, 2 November.

Kuypers, J.A. (2009). 'Framing Analysis', in Kuypers, J.A., ed. *Rhetorical Criticism: Perspectives in Action*. Lanham, MD: Lexington Books.

Labaton, S. (1999a). 'House to Debate Financial Overhaul Law Today'. *The New York Times*, 1 July.

Labaton, S. (1999b). 'Bill to Overhaul Financial System Passes the House'. *The New York Times*, 2 July.

Labaton, S. (1999c). 'Republicans Propose a Deal on Financial Services'. *The New York Times*, 12 October.

Labaton, S. (1999d). 'Lawmakers Reject Clinton Changes to Finance-Overhaul Bill'. *The New York Times*, 15 October.

Labaton, S. (1999e). 'Congress Passes Wide-ranging Bill Easing Bank Laws'. *The New York Times*, 5 November.

Labaton, S. (2009a). 'Obama Enlisted Broad Consensus on Finance Rules'. *The New York Times*, 17 June.

Labaton, S. (2009b). 'Leading Senator Pushes New Plan to Oversee Banks', *The New York Times*, 21 September.

Labaton, S. and Stout, D. (2009). 'Vote Backs a Financial Oversight Body'. *The New York Times*, 23 October.

Levendusky, M. (2013). *How Partisan Media Polarize America*. Chicago, IL: University of Chicago Press.

Lewis, M. (2010). *The Big Short: Inside the Doomsday Machine*. London: W.W. Norton and Company.

Lo, A.W. (2012). 'Reading about the Financial Crisis: A Twenty-One-Book Review'. *Journal of Economic Literature*, 50(1), 151–178.

López, A.M.R. and Llopis, M.Á.O. (2010). 'Metaphorical Pattern Analysis in Financial Texts: Framing the Crisis in Positive or Negative Metaphorical Terms'. *Journal of Pragmatics*, 42(12), 3300–3313.

Luntz, F. (2010). *The Language of Financial Reform*. The Word Doctors.

Mackinac Center for Public Policy. (2020). *The Overton Window*.

Manning, P. (2013). 'Financial Journalism, News Sources and the Banking Crisis'. *Journalism*, 14(2), 173–189.

Marron, M.B., Sarabia-Panol, Z., Sison, M.D., Rao, S. and Niekamp, R. (2010). 'The Scorecard on Reporting of the Global Financial Crisis'. *Journalism Studies*, 11(2), 270–283.

Matthes, J. (2009). 'What's in a Frame? A Content Analysis of Media Framing Studies in the World's Leading Communication Journals 1990–2005'. *Journalism & Mass Communication Quarterly*, 86(2), 349–367.

Mayer, J. (2021). 'Inside the Koch-Backed Effort to Block the Largest Election Reform Bill in Half a Century'. *The New Yorker*, 29 March.

McBeth, M.K., Shanahan, E.A., Arnell, R.J. and Hathaway, P.L. (2007). 'The Intersection of Narrative Policy Analysis and Policy Change Theory'. *Policy Studies Journal*, 35(1), 87–108.

McBeth, M.K., Tokle, R.J. and Schaefer, S. (2018). 'Media Narratives Versus Evidence in Economic Policy Making: The 2008–2009 Financial Crisis'. *Social Science Quarterly*, 99(2), 179–806.

McChesney, R.W. and Nichols, J. (2010). *The Death and Life of American Journalism: The Media Revolution That Will Begin the World Again*. Philadelphia, PA: Nation Books.

McCombs, M. (2005). 'A Look at Agenda-Setting: Past, Present and Future'. *Journalism Studies*, 6(4), 543–557.

McCombs, M. and Shaw, D. (1972). 'The Agenda-Setting Function of Mass Media'. *Public Opinion Quarterly*, 36(2), 176–187.

McCulley, P. (2009). 'The Shadow Banking System and Hyman Minsky's Economic Journey'. *Global Central Bank Focus*, 12, 257–268.

McGann, J.G. (2009). 'Global Go To Think Tank Index Report'. TTCSP Global Go To Think Tank Index Reports.

McGann, J.G. (2010). 'Global Go To Think Tank Index Report'. TTCSP Global Go To Think Tank Index Reports.

McGann, J.G. (2011). 'Global Go To Think Tank Index Report'. TTCSP Global Go To Think Tank Index Reports.

McGann, J.G. (2012). 'Global Go To Think Tank Index Report'. TTCSP Global Go To Think Tank Index Reports.

Mehran, H., Morrison, A. and Shapiro, J. (2011). 'Corporate Governance and Banks: What Have We Learned from the Financial Crisis?'. Staff Report, Federal Reserve Bank of New York.

Meraz, S. (2009). 'Is There an Elite Hold? Traditional Media to Social Media Agenda Setting Influence in Blog Networks'. *Journal of Computer-Mediated Communication*, 14(3), 682–707.

Merle, R. (2010). 'Push Would Limit Power of States to Enforce Consumer Protection; Lawmakers, Firms Seek to Leave Authority with Proposed Federal Bureau'. *The Washington Post*, 15 May.

Merton, R. (1936). 'The Unanticipated Consequences of Purposive Social Action'. *American Sociological Review*, 1(6), 894–904.

Mill, J.S. (1844) 'Essays on Some Unsettled Questions of Political Economy'. London: John W. Parker.

Miller, M.M. and Riechert, B.P. (2001). 'The Spiral of Opportunity and Frame Resonance: Mapping the Issue Cycle in News and Public Discourse', in Reese, S.D., Gandy, O.H. and Grant, A.E., eds. *Framing Public Life: Perspectives on Media and Our Understanding of the Social World*. Mahwah, NJ: Lawrence Erlbaum Associates, Inc.

Minsky, H. (1992). 'The Financial Instability Hypothesis'. Working Paper 74, Jerome Levy Economics Institute, Annandale on Hudson, New York.

Mohamed, S. (2009). 'Cheerleaders to a Crisis: The Global Financial Crisis'. *Rhodes Journalism Review*, 29, 14–16.

Morgan, D.P. and Stiroh, K.J. (2005). 'Too Big to Fail After All These Years'. Federal Reserve Bank of New York Staff Report No. 220, September.

Morgenson, G. (2011). 'Slipping Backward on Swaps'. *The New York Times*, 27 November.

Nakamoto, M. and Wighton, D. (2007). 'Citigroup Chief Stays Bullish on Buy-Outs'. *Financial Times*, 9 July.

New York Times. (1999). 'A New World of Finance'. *The New York Times*, 24 October.

Norris, F. (2010). 'A Baby Step Towards Rules on Bank Risk'. *The New York Times*, 17 September.

Office of the Clerk of the U.S. House of Representatives. (1999). Final Vote Results for Roll Call 570.

Pagliari, S. (2013). *Public Salience and International Financial Regulation. Explaining the International Regulation of OTC Derivatives, Rating Agencies, and Hedge Funds*. PhD Thesis, University of Waterloo.

Parliament. House of Commons (2009). *Bank Nationalisation Report*.

Pearce, R.G. (1995). 'The Professionalism Paradigm Shift: Why Discarding Professional Ideology Will Improve the Conduct and Reputation of the Bar'. *New York University Law Review*, 70(6), 1229–1276.

Peck, J. (2008). 'Remaking Laissez-Faire'. *Progress in Human Geography*, 32(1), 3–43.

Perry, M.J. and Dell, R. (2010). 'How Government Failure Caused the Great Recession'. American Enterprise Institute.

Pew Research Center. (2012). *Auto Bailout Now Backed, Stimulus Divided*.

Pierce, A. (2008). 'The Queen Asks Why No One Saw the Credit Crunch Coming'. *The Telegraph*, 5 November.

Polanyi, K. (1957). *The Great Transformation*. Boston: Beacon Press.

Public Broadcasting Service. (2008). 'President Urges Congress to Take 'Decisive Action' on Bailout'. Public Broadcasting Service, 30 September.

Quiggan, J. (2010). *Zombie Economics: How Dead Ideas Still Walk among Us*. Princeton, NJ: Princeton University Press.

Rahn, R. (2010). 'What Caused the Financial Crisis'. Cato Institute.

Reagan, R. (1981). 'Ronald Reagan Inaugural Address'. *The American Presidency Project*.

Reinhart, C.M. and Rogoff, K.S. (2009). *This Time is Different*. Princeton, NJ: Princeton University Press.

Retirement Topics – 401(k) and Profit-Sharing Plan Contribution Limits 2020.

Rogers, E.M. and Dearing, J.W. (1988). 'Agenda-Setting Research: Where Has It Been? Where Is It Going?', in Anderson, J.A., ed. *Communication Yearbook* 11. Newbury Park, CA: Sage.

Roosevelt, F.D. (1936). Speech Given at Madison Square Garden, New York City, 31 October. FDR Library website.

Rosen, J. (2009). 'He Said, She Said Journalism: Lame Formula in the Land of the Active User'. *Press Think.*

Roush, C. (2009). 'Unheeded Warnings'. *American Journalism Review*, December–January.

Russell, N.J. (2006). 'An Introduction to the Overton Window of Political Possibilities'. *Students for a Free Economy Clarkson Colloquium.*

Schechter, D. (2009). 'Credit Crisis: How Did We Miss It?'. *British Journalism Review*, 20(1), 19–26.

Scheufele, D.A. (1999). 'Framing as a Theory of Media Effects'. *Journal of Communication*, 49(1), 103–122.

Schiffrin, A. (2011). 'The U.S. Press and the Financial Crisis', in Schiffrin, A., ed. *The US Press and the Financial Crisis. Bad News: How America's Business Press Missed the Story of the Century.* New York, NY: New Press.

Schiffrin, A. (2015). 'The Press and the Financial Crisis: A Review of the Literature'. *Sociology Compass*, 9(8), 639–653.

Schlesinger, A.M. (1958). *The Age of Roosevelt. Volume II (1933–1935): The Coming of the New Deal.* Boston, MA: Houghton Mifflin.

Schranz, M. and Eisenegger, M. (2011). 'The Media Construction of the Financial Crisis in a Comparative Perspective – An Analysis of Newspapers in the UK, USA and Switzerland between 2007 and 2009'. *Swiss Journal of Sociology*, 37(2), 241–258.

Schudson, M. (2001). 'The Objectivity Norm in American Journalism'. *Journalism*, 2(2), 149–170.

Schumpeter, J.A. (1942). *Capitalism, Socialism, and Democracy.* New York, NY: Harper and Row.

Sen, S. (2010). 'The Meltdown of the Global Economy: A Keynes-Minsky Episode?'. Working Paper No. 623. Annandale-on-Hudson, NY: The Levy Economics Institute of Bard College.

Shearmur, J. (1997). 'Hayek, Keynes and the State'. *History of Economics Review*, 26(1), 68–82.

Sim, Y., Acree, B.D.L., Gross, J.H. and Smith, N.A. (2013). 'Measuring Ideological Proportions in Political Speeches', in *Proceedings of the 2013 Conference on Empirical Methods in Natural Language Processing.* Presented at the EMNLP 2013. Seattle, WA: Association for Computational Linguistics, 91–101.

Skidelsky, R.J.A. (2003). *John Maynard Keynes 1883–1946: Economist, Philosopher, Statesman.* London and Basingstoke: Macmillan.

Skovsgaard, M., Albæk, E., Bro, P. and de Vreese, C. (2013). 'A Reality Check: How Journalists' Role Perceptions Impact Their Implementation of the Objectivity Norm'. *Journalism*, 14(1), 22–42.

Slate. (2018). *Regulate Me: The Financial Crisis Continues to Linger* [podcast], 8 August 2018.

Sorkin, A.R. (2009). *Too Big to Fail: The Inside Story of How Wall Street and Washington Fought to Save the Financial System – and Themselves.* New York, NY: Viking.

Sorkin, A.R. (2016). 'President Obama Weighs His Economic Legacy'. *The New York Times Magazine*, 28 April.

Splichal, S. (1999). *Public Opinion: Developments and Controversies in the Twentieth Century*. Lanham, MD: Rowman & Littlefield.

Starkman, D. (2014). *The Watchdog that Didn't Bark*. New York, NY: Columbia University Press.

States News Service (2009). *Frank Delivers Major Speech on Financial Regulation at National Press Club* [press release]. 27 July.

Stein, S. (2010). 'Frank Luntz Pens Memo to Kill Regulatory Reform'. *The Huffington Post*, 3 April.

Stewart, J.B. (2009). 'Eight Days'. *The New Yorker*, 21 September.

Stiglitz, J.E. (1993). 'The Role of the State in Financial Markets', in *Proceedings of the World Bank Conference on Development Economics*. Washington, DC: World Bank.

Stiglitz, J.E. (2014). 'The Media and the Crisis. An Information Theoretic Approach', in Schifferes, S. and Roberts, R., eds. *The Media and Financial Crises: Comparative and Historical Perspective*. London: Routledge.

Stone, D. (2002). *Policy Paradox: The Art of Political Decision Making*, Revised Edition. New York, NY: W.W. Norton and Company.

Stone, O. and Pressman, E.R. (1987). *Wall Street* [Motion Picture]. United States: Twentieth Century Fox Film Corporation.

Strömbäck, J., Aalberg, T. and Jenssen, A. (2010). 'News Coverage of the Financial Crisis and Public Perception of Government Regulation'. APSA 2010 Annual Meeting Paper.

Tambini, D. (2008). *What Is Financial Journalism for? Ethics and Responsibility in a Time of Crisis and Change*. London: Polis and the London School of Economics.

Tankard, J., Hendrickson, L., Silberman, J., Bliss, K. and Ghanem, S. (1991). 'Media Frames: Approaches to Conceptualization and Measurement'. Paper presented to the Association for Education in Journalism and Mass Communication conference, Boston, MA.

Taylor, C.R. (2018). 'The Dodd-Frank Death Knell'. *Loyola University Chicago Law Journal*, 49(3), 655–668.

Time. (1965). 'The economy: We Are All Keynesians now'. *Time*, 31 December.

The American Prospect (2021). 'About the Prospect'. American Prospect. Available at: https://prospect.org/about

The Harris Poll. (2012). *Most People Oppose Bailouts, but a Sizable Plurality of the Public Believes that the 2009 Bailout of the Car Industry Helped the Economy*. Harris Insight & Analytics LLC.

The Mont Pèlerin Society. (2020). *Statement of Aims*. https://www.montpelerin.org/statement-of-aims/ (accessed 15 December 2021).

The Word Doctors. (n.d.). LinkedIn page. https://www.linkedin.com/company/the-word-doctors/about/ (accessed 15 December 2021).

Tse, T.M. (2009). 'Wall St. Jacks Up Pay After Bailouts; Lawmakers Warn Against Return to Pre-Crisis Levels'. *The Washington Post*, 23 July.

Tung, F. (2011). 'Pay for Banker Performance: Structuring Executive Compensation for Risk Regulation'. *Northwestern University Law Review*, 105(3), 1205–1252.

United States Senate. (1999). *Roll Call Vote 106th Congress – 1st Session.*

United States Senate Committee on Banking, Housing and Urban Affairs. (2008). 'Turmoil in U.S. Credit Markets: Examining the Recent Actions of Federal Financial Regulators'. 3 April.

Usher, N. (2013). 'Ignored, Uninterested, and the Blame Game: How *The New York Times*, *Marketplace*, and The Street Distanced Themselves from Preventing the 2007–2009 Financial Crisis'. *Journalism*, 14(2), 190–207.

U.S. House Committee on Banking, Finance and Urban Affairs. (1984).

U.S. House Committee on Financial Services. (2009a). *Perspectives on Systemic Risk*, 5 March. Washington: Government Printing Office.

U.S. House Committee on Financial Services. (2009b). *Perspectives on Regulation of Systemic Risk in the Financial Services Industry*, 17 March. Washington: Government Printing Office.

U.S. House Committee on Financial Services. (2009c). *Systemic Regulation, Prudential Matters, Resolution Authority, and Securitization*, 29 October. Washington: Government Printing Office.

Wall Street Journal CEO Council. (2008). 'Rahm Emanuel on the Opportunities of Crisis'. 19 November.

Wallison, P.J. (2012). 'Breaking Up the Big Banks: Is Anybody Thinking?' American Enterprise Institute.

Watts, M.D., Domke, D., Shah, D.V. and Fan, D.P. (1999). 'Elite Cues and Media Bias in Presidential Campaigns'. *Communication Research*, 26(2), 144–175.

Weitzner, D. and Darroch, J. (2009). 'Why Moral Failures Precede Financial Crises'. *Critical Perspectives on International Business*, 5(1–2), 6–13.

White House Office of the Press Secretary. (2010). *Remarks by the President on Financial Reform.*

Wingfield, B. (2009). 'Spencer Bachus on Rethinking Regulation'. *Forbes*, 21 September.

Wyatt, E. (2011a). 'Fed Chief Says U.S. Has Bolstered Its Ability to Handle Failure of a Big Bank'. *The New York Times*, 18 February.

Wyatt, E. (2011b). 'To Cushion Against Losses, Fed Considers Raising Capital Requirements for Banks'. *The New York Times*, 4 June.

Wyatt, E. and Herszenhorn, D.M. (2010). 'Bill on Finance Wins Approval of Senate Panel'. *The New York Times*, 22 April.

Yang, J.L. (2010). 'Panel Scraps Bank Fee in Financial Overhaul; Democrats Reopen Negotiations to Keep Key Republican Support'. *The Washington Post*, 30 June.

Index

For Product Safety Concerns and Information please contact our EU
representative GPSR@taylorandfrancis.com
Taylor & Francis Verlag GmbH, Kaufingerstraße 24, 80331 München, Germany

9 7 8 1 0 3 2 0 1 2 6 4 3